OECD Public Governance Reviews

Trafficking in Persons and Corruption

BREAKING THE CHAIN

Please cite this publication as:
OECD (2016), *Trafficking in Persons and Corruption: Breaking the Chain*, OECD Public Governance Reviews, OECD Publishing, Paris.
http://dx.doi.org/10.1787/9789264253728-en

ISBN 978-92-64-25371-1 (print)
ISBN 978-92-64-25372-8 (PDF)

Series: OECD Public Governance Reviews
ISSN 2219-0406 (print)
ISSN 2219-0414 (online)

Photo credits: Cover © Stocksnapper - Fotolia.com.

Corrigenda to OECD publications may be found on line at: *www.oecd.org/about/publishing/corrigenda.htm*.

Foreword

Over 20 million people are estimated to be victims of forced labour globally, which includes victims of trafficking for forced labour and sexual exploitation. While considerable steps have been taken by governments across the world to combat this multi-billion-dollar business that is destroying lives and violating fundamental human rights, the impact on the ground remains limited. At the same time, the proceeds of traffickers continue to rise. In light of the current refugee crisis, combatting trafficking in persons and ensuring that more people do not become victims is more relevant than ever. Adults and unaccompanied minors alike who have been forced to flee their home countries in search of safety, political stability and humane living conditions are particularly vulnerable to exploitation. They arrive in a new and unfamiliar country without possessions, and in need of physical and economic security.

Trafficking in persons (TIP) relies on systemic corruption. Corruption ensures that traffickers can operate undisturbed and under the radar, without risk of being arrested or convicted even when a trafficking crime has been uncovered. It also allows for the re-trafficking of victims that were able to escape their situation of exploitation. Corrupt behaviour ranges from active involvement, such as violating duties, accepting or transferring bribes, and facilitating transactions, to passive involvement, such as ignoring or failing to follow up on information that a crime may be taking place, and is present throughout the trafficking chain.

Yet, what has largely been missing in the current efforts to address trafficking in persons is a comprehensive analysis of how corruption facilitates trafficking and how interventions could be leveraged, re-focused, or introduced to more effectively reach the desired results within both areas.

Recognising the need to strengthen the anti-corruption component in the efforts to address this acute humanitarian challenge, the OECD has developed "Guiding Principles on Combatting Corruption related to Trafficking in Persons". These Guiding Principles have gone through multiple rounds of consultation and were field-tested in the Philippines and Thailand to ensure that they focus on "what works" and capture the knowledge and lessons learned that have been accumulated by the experts from national governments, civil society and academia.

These Guiding Principles are part of the OECD's efforts to analyse the role that corruption plays in facilitating globalised illegal activities, such as human trafficking, terrorism, illicit trade, and organised crime. Only by having a comprehensive and cohesive approach to strengthen institutions and target the corrupt links in these activities can policy makers break the chain and advance into combatting global threats.

Acknowledgements

This report was prepared by the Public Sector Integrity Division of the OECD Directorate for Public Governance and Territorial Development.

Under the guidance of Janos Bertók, the research, co-ordination and drafting of this report was conducted by Ulrika Bonnier. Invaluable input and guidance was provided by Julio Bacio Terracino.

The OECD expresses its gratitude to the US Department of State for its support for this project. Special thanks go to the participants of the APEC Pathfinder Dialogue II on "Strengthening the Fight Against Corruption and Illicit Trade – Partnerships for Sustainable Security" that took place in Cebu City on 26 August 2015; the OECD Roundtable on Combatting Corruption related to Trafficking in Persons that took place in Cebu City on 27 August 2015; and the meetings of the OECD Task Force on Charting Illicit Trade and the OECD Working Party of Senior Public Integrity Officials where this report and the "Guiding Principles on Combatting Corruption related to Trafficking in Persons" have been discussed.

The OECD would also like to thank the American Bar Association for their feedback on the Guiding Principles, and the government agencies and non-governmental organisations that participated in the consultations during the OECD fact-finding mission to the Philippines and Thailand in August 2015, namely: Ateneo de Manila University, the Center Against International Human Trafficking at the Office of the Attorney General of Thailand, the Department of Justice of the Philippines, ECPAT, the Exodus Road, the Inter-Agency Council Against Trafficking of the Philippines, the Ministry of Social Development and Human Security of Thailand, the Office of the Civil Service Commission of Thailand, the Office of the National Anti-Corruption Commission of Thailand, the Office of the Public Sector Development Commission of Thailand, the Philippine National Police, the Philippine Overseas Employment Agency, PREDA, the Royal Thai Police, Transparency International Philippines, and the Visayan Forum Foundation.

Table of contents

Tables

Figures

Executive summary

Trafficking in persons (TIP) violates many of the most fundamental human rights and is present throughout all regions of the world. It is also one of the most lucrative forms of organised crime. The International Labour Organization (ILO) estimates that 20.9 million people are victims of forced labour globally and that the total illicit profits produced by trafficked forced labourers are about USD 150 billion per year.

Organised trafficking requires systematic corruption. Trafficking in persons would not be as prevalent and widespread if it were not for the leverage supplied by corruption, and human trafficking could not occur on the scale it does if it were not for the complicity and collusion of corrupt officials with criminal gangs. This publication explores the links between corruption and TIP with a specific focus on mitigating corruption risks and applying a sound integrity framework for preventing corruption related to trafficking in persons.

While considerable steps have been taken to combat trafficking in persons, these have not comprehensively focused on the fundamental role that corruption plays in the trafficking process. The approach of addressing these two issues jointly – coupled with better cross-border co-operation, better enforcement and an increased focus on combatting corruption – is key to effectively curb trafficking in persons. The OECD has therefore developed "Guiding Principles on Combatting Corruption related to Trafficking in Persons". The purpose of these principles is to provide reference for countries intending to establish, modify or complement a framework to address TIP-related corruption.

The Guiding Principles recognise the need to embrace a comprehensive approach against corruption related to trafficking in persons and for this reason they cover a broad range of equally important issues in the realm of prevention and enforcement. Solid legal bases are a fundamental starting point for tackling TIP-related corruption. Relevant international agreements already provide a common basis, which should guide countries in their efforts to strengthen their legal framework and intensify international co-operation. However, in order to face the fact that both international instruments and domestic legislation often consider corruption and trafficking separately; the principles stress the importance of designing new mechanisms and strategies – or revise existing ones – to address and investigate the two issues in a coherent and co-ordinated way. The latter efforts should target with particular emphasis the sectors and industries that are most vulnerable to TIP, such as the construction, brothel, agriculture, fishing and textile industries. In parallel, specific rules and standards of transparency and integrity should be designed for those public officials who are most exposed to the risk of being involved in trafficking and corruption. Furthermore, the principles encourage the implementation of preventive measures as well as awareness-raising activities that focus on the linkages between corruption and trafficking in persons – especially among parties involved in anti-trafficking issues and potential victims of trafficking. At the same time, the principles recognise that any strategy against TIP-related corruption should be complemented by a better understanding of the phenomenon. Efforts and resources should therefore be dedicated to improving the collection of data and the use of information collected by non-governmental organisations (NGOs).

In August 2015, the practical application of the Guiding Principles was tested in the Philippines and Thailand. Based on the gap analysis that was conducted, as well as the feedback received from government agencies and non-governmental actors, the Guiding Principles were found to be both useful and relevant for addressing trafficking-in-persons-related corruption. Stakeholders highlighted the Guiding Principles' joint approach to trafficking and corruption as a particular strong point, and emphasised that the principles' detailed nature, with the inclusion of specific examples on how to implement the different recommendations, was particularly useful. In sum, the testing of the Guiding Principles showed that they not only reflect many of the good practices that country representatives highlighted, but that they also raise recommendations in areas where more work is needed to effectively address trafficking-in-persons-related corruption. The Guiding Principles – as reflected in the boxes in case study Chapters 4 and 5, as well as Chapter 3 of this report where they are introduced – have been revised to take into account the feedback received from the in-country consultations.

Throughout the consultations conducted, stakeholders suggested that a collection of best practices from a wide range of countries could be useful, and could assist them in identifying potential measures that could help address the challenges that they face in relation to trafficking-in-persons-related corruption. Moving forward, the collection of specific examples and best practices could therefore be expanded further – and in a larger sample of countries.

A brief summary of the "Guiding Principles on Combatting Corruption related to Trafficking in Persons"

1. International co-operation and agreements
   - Relevant international conventions are ratified and international co-operation against corruption and trafficking in persons is promoted.
   - Processes of international co-operation in terms of mutual legal assistance and extradition are in place and functioning.
2. Jointly addressing and investigating trafficking in persons and corruption with particular focus on at-risk sectors
   - Strategies that address trafficking in persons and corruption, or include corruption issues in anti-trafficking plans, and vice versa, are in place.
   - Sectors prone to trafficking-in-persons-related corruption are given priority in the implementation of relevant strategies.
   - Information and resources are leveraged and shared among relevant actors.
   - Corruption is also investigated when investigating trafficking in persons.
   - Specialised multi-agency units are established and multi-agency trainings are organised.

A brief summary of the "Guiding Principles on Combatting Corruption related to Trafficking in Persons" *(continued)*

3. Transparency and an integrity framework for public officials at risk
   - Specific rules/standards of behaviour – such as guidelines or codes of conduct – with respect to corruption and trafficking for public officials at risk are in place. The violations of the codes of conduct entail sanctions.
   - The activities of staff working in sectors at risk are performed in a transparent manner.
   - A wider framework of integrity for public officials is promoted.
   - Mechanisms that allow for public officials as well as the public to expose misconduct and report dishonest or illegal activity and that ensure the effective protection from retaliation are in place.
   - The recruitment process of officials is transparent, competitive and subject to independent scrutiny. Upon recruitment, officials receive training, adequate supervision and are subject to regular performance evaluations.
   - Key officials receive training so that they are able to correctly identify trafficking victims, understand the nature of the crime, and recognise warning signs throughout the different stages of the trafficking-in-persons process.
4. Awareness-raising and prevention measures for public officials and the general public
   - Public awareness regarding the existence, causes, and gravity of trafficking in persons and the active participation of individuals and groups outside the public sector in the prevention of and the fight against trafficking-in-persons-related corruption is promoted.
   - Targeted awareness-raising measures for all parties involved in anti-trafficking issues are provided.
   - Preventive measures for potential victims of trafficking in persons are in place, in particular offering counselling about corruption and trafficking before and after they have undertaken a migration journey and alerting communities of early signs of corruption.
5. Improvement of data collection and systematic use of information
   - Data on trafficking in persons are collected, analysed and used systematically.
6. Lift immunity in corruption and trafficking cases
   - Immunity from prosecution of public officials is duly lifted to allow for effective investigation, prosecution and adjudication of corruption and trafficking-in-persons-related offences.

Chapter 1

Trafficking in persons: Weak governance and growing profits

This chapter explores one of the most lucrative forms of organised crime: trafficking in persons. It focuses on the magnitude of the crime in terms of both profit and the number of victims, the transnational nature of trafficking in persons, and takes stock of progress in enforcement of the anti-trafficking laws in place. In addition, the chapter presents a number of efforts that have been made to combat trafficking in persons in terms of international and regional conventions, legislation from national governments and private sector initiatives.

Illicit trade is a multi-billion-dollar business (Table 1.1) and an increasing concern for countries. It ranges from trade in counterfeit pharmaceuticals, electronics and cigarettes to, among other things, trade in drugs, wildlife, and humans. From an economic perspective, all these activities divert money from governments' tax revenue and the balance sheets of legitimate businesses and put cash in the hands of criminals, who build larger illicit networks (see, e.g. Luna, 2012). Illicit trade threatens the level playing field, economic growth, sustainable development, social cohesion, security and stability. Since illicit trade is a global problem, it cannot be solved by individual governments. Instead, bilateral, regional and international co-operation and initiatives are needed.

Table 1.1. **Estimated value of illicit international trade, 2011**

Market	Estimated value of illicit international trade
Drugs	USD 320 billion
Humans	USD 31.6 billion
Wildlife	USD 7.8-10 billion
Counterfeit total	USD 250 billion
Counterfeit pharmaceuticals	USD 35-40 billion
Counterfeit electronics	USD 50 billion
Counterfeit cigarettes	USD 2.6 billion
Human organs	USD 614 million to USD 1.2 billion
Small arms and light weapons	USD 300 million to USD 1 billion
Diamonds and colored gemstones	USD 860 million
Oil	USD 10.8 billion
Timber	USD 7 billion
Fish	USD 4.2-9.5 billion
Art and cultural property	USD 3.4-6.3 billion
Gold	USD 2.3 billion
Total	**USD 639-651 billion**
Approximation	**USD 650 billion**

Note: In 2015, the International Labour Organization published a new estimate of the total illicit profits produced in one year by trafficked forced labourers. This new estimate of USD 150 billion was not available during the time of publication of the study that the above table references. The table should therefore only be used as an indication of the relative values of the different markets of illicit trade, and not as a reference in relation to the absolute amounts.

Source: Haken, J. (2011). *Transnational Crime in The Developing World*, Global Financial Integrity, Washington, DC, p. 56, www.gfintegrity.org/storage/gfip/documents/reports/transcrime/gfi_transnational_crime_web.pdf.

The UN Trafficking in Persons Protocol defines the crime of trafficking in persons as consisting of 1) *acts* such as recruitment, transport, transfer, harbouring, receipt of a person, by 2) *means* of abduction, fraud, deception, coercion, abuse of power or a position of vulnerability and others for the 3) *purpose of exploitation*, including sexual exploitation, forced labour, and the removal of organs.[1] Trafficking in persons differs from smuggling of migrants, which refers to "the procurement, in order to obtain, directly or indirectly, a financial or other material benefit, of the illegal entry of a person into a State Party of which the person is not a national or a permanent resident" ("Protocol Against the Smuggling of Migrants by Land, Sea and Air") – with its focus on illegal border crossings. Trafficking in persons instead centres around human rights violations through exploitation, most commonly the right to personal autonomy, the right not to be held in slavery or servitude, the right to liberty and security of persons, the right to be free from cruel or inhumane treatment, the right to safe and healthy working conditions and the freedom of movement (GTZ, 2008). However, in practice, it is not uncommon that what starts off as smuggling of migrants can turn into a situation of human trafficking. For example, a pre-determined fee for entering a country illegally can – once the border crossing has been completed – be raised to an amount that the migrant cannot afford. In order to pay off this increased fee, and under threats from the smuggler to report the migrant's illegal border entry to the authorities, the migrant can end up in a situation of forced labour or sexual exploitation, making this person a victim of trafficking.

Trafficking in persons has become one of the most lucrative forms of organised crime (Table 1.1) (see, e.g. Shelley, 2010). It is estimated that trafficking in persons and slavery is the third most lucrative illicit business in the world after arms and drugs trafficking (Arlacchi, 2000). ILO estimates that the total illicit profits produced per year by trafficked forced labourers are about USD 150 billion (Table 1.2). Out of these USD 150 billion, forced sexual exploitation is estimated to generate USD 99 billion per year, and forced labour exploitation, including domestic work, agriculture and other economic activities, an estimated USD 51 billion (ILO, 2015).

Table 1.2. **Estimated average annual profits generated by trafficked forced labourers**

	Annual profit per victim of forced labour per region (USD)	Annual profits of forced labour per region (USD billions)
Asia-Pacific	5 000	51.8
Developed economies and European Union	34 800	46.9
Central and South-Eastern Europe and CIS	12 900	18.0
Africa	3 900	13.1
Latin America and the Caribbean	7 500	12.0
Middle East	15 000	8.5
World		≈150

Source: ILO. (2015), *Profits and Poverty: The Economics of Forced Labour*, ILO, Geneva, p. 14.

According to the International Labour Organization (ILO), 20.9 million people are victims of forced labour[2] globally (ILO, 2012). At the EU level, data from the 2015 edition of the Eurostat report on statistics on trafficking in human beings shows that 30 146 victims were registered in the 28 EU Member States between 2010 and 2012. Some 80% of these victims were female, and 69% of the total number of victims registered were trafficked for sexual exploitation (Eurostat, 2015).

Trafficking in persons is often transnational in nature, with 66% of trafficking victims being trafficked across borders. However, 40% of detected victims are trafficked from a country in the same region as the country of destination or from a nearby subregion, and only about a quarter (26%) are trafficked across different regions (UNODC, 2014). Between 2010 and 2012, 97% of detected victims in the East Asia and Pacific region were from within the region or the country (Figure 1.1). Eurostat data also supports this finding. Between 2010 and 2012, 65% of registered victims in the European Union were EU citizens (Eurostat, 2015). This finding would support a focus on regional co-operation to combat TIP, with the exception of North Africa and the Middle East.

Figure 1.1. **Share of detected victims who were trafficked within or from outside the region, 2010-12**

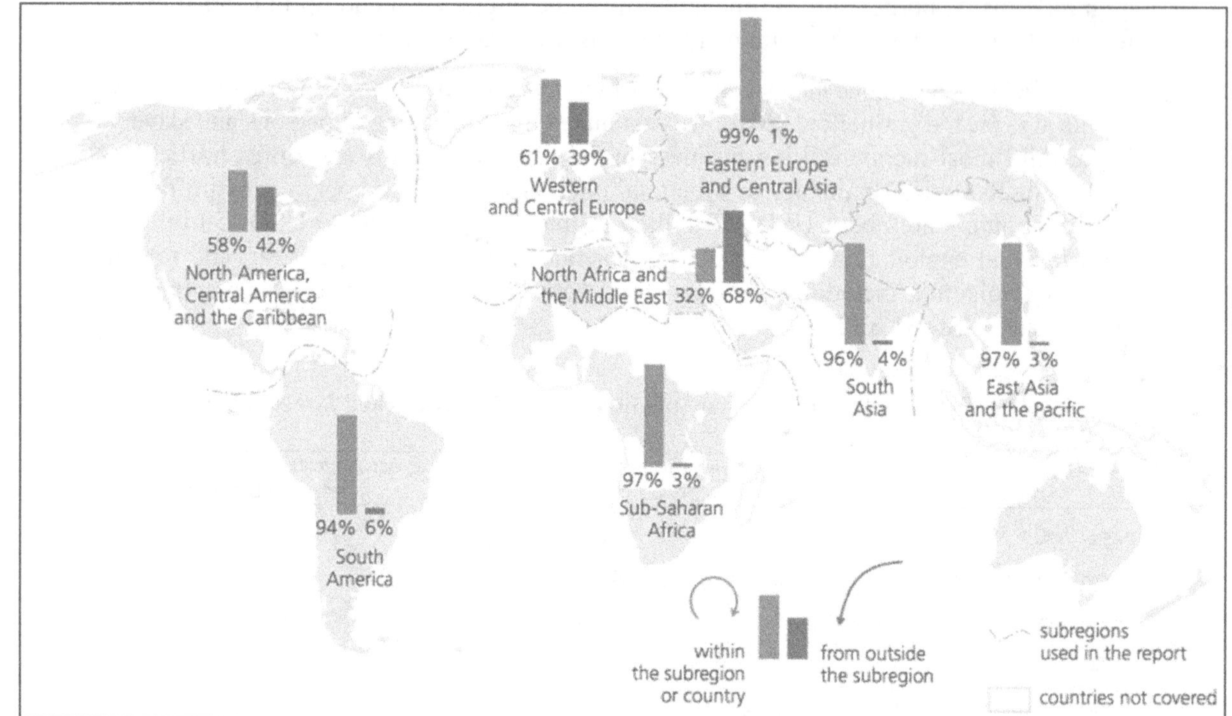

Source: UNODC (2014), *Global Report on Trafficking in Persons 2014*, United Nations, New York, p. 39, www.unodc.org/documents/data-and-analysis/glotip/GLOTIP_2014_full_report.pdf.

Of 173 countries covered by the UNODC's *Global Report on Trafficking in Persons 2014,* 146 countries had a specific offence in their domestic legislation covering most or all forms of trafficking in persons. However, 9 countries had no legislation in place, and 18 countries had partial legislation in place, leaving 2 billion people without the full protection of the Trafficking in Persons Protocol (UNODC, 2014).

Despite the evident global concern over trafficking in persons, progress in enforcement remains limited. According to the UNODC (2014), 15% of the countries that have included TIP as a specific offense did not record a single conviction in the period 2010-12. Similar trends were recorded in the period 2007-10 (see Figure 1.2). In the European Union, Eurostat data show that 8 805 prosecutions for trafficking in human beings were reported between 2010 and 2012 in the European Union, with 2 855 convictions (Eurostat, 2015).

Figure 1.2. **Number of trafficking convictions recorded per year, 2007-10**

Percentage of countries

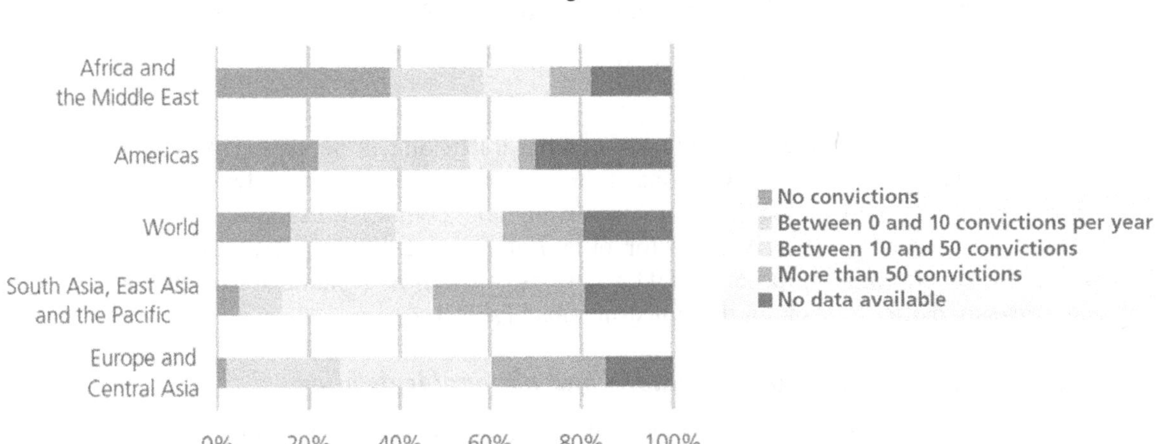

Source: UNODC (2012), *Global Report on Trafficking* in Persons *2012,* United Nations, New York, p. 86, www.unodc.org/unodc/en/data-and-analysis/glotip_2012.html.

The US Department of State collects worldwide data on trafficking prosecutions, convictions and sentences and estimates that in 2014 there were 10 051 prosecutions and 4 443 convictions globally (Table 1.3). The low conviction rate overall reveals difficulty in successfully prosecuting the underlying offenses. In addition, the low ratio of prosecutions to number of victims identified could imply that some regions are particularly inactive - although this low ratio could also be explained by traffickers in these regions victimising a higher volume of persons.

Table 1.3. **Law enforcement data by region, 2014**

	Prosecutions	Convictions	Victims identified
Africa	811 (49)	317 (33)	9 523 (1 308)
East Asia and Pacific	1 938 (88)	969 (16)	6 349 (1 084)
Europe	4 199 (197)	1 585 (69)	11 910 (3 531)
Near East	320 (5)	144 (25)	3 388 (2 460)
South and Central Asia	1 839 (12)	958 (10)	4 878 (1 041)
Western Hemisphere	944 (67)	470 (63)	8 414 (2 014)
Global	10 051 (418)	4 443 (216)	44 462 (11 438)

Note: The above statistics are estimates only, given the lack of uniformity in national reporting structures. The numbers in parentheses are those of labour trafficking prosecutions, convictions, and victims identified. The number of victims identified includes information from foreign governments and other sources.

Source: US Department of State (2015), *Trafficking in Persons Report July 2015*, US Department of State, Washington, DC, pp. 55-60.

The data that are collected worldwide by non-governmental organisations (NGOs) and the different national and local agencies tasked with working on trafficking in persons need to be systematically collected, aggregated, and shared at both the national and regional level. The availability of this information would make it possible to strengthen policies designed to prevent trafficking and protect victims, increase prosecutions, and evaluate whether the money invested to combat human trafficking has had the desired impact or could be better spent in the future. An economic analysis could provide insights into the functioning of trafficking markets for persons, and where policy interventions could usefully undermine the prevailing incentive structures. Donors and governments need to know what public policies work and what has proven sub-optimal.

Efforts to combat trafficking in persons

Considerable steps have been taken to combat trafficking in persons. One approach has been to adopt a series of conventions at the international and regional level as well as several pieces of national legislation to prevent and combat trafficking in persons. Similarly, in recent years, private sector organisations and civil society have adopted initiatives for the same purpose. OECD countries, as well as a number of non-OECD countries, are parties to many of these instruments (Table 1. 4).

International and regional conventions and national legislation

This section provides a brief overview of the main instruments developed to prevent and combat trafficking in persons. The main international and regional instruments – as well as a selection of national instruments – that deal specifically with the subject of trafficking in persons or the issue of forced labour are found below.

The United Nations Trafficking in Persons Protocol

The "United Nations Convention against Transnational Organized Crime", adopted by General Assembly resolution 55/25 of 15 November 2000, was opened for signature by Member States in Palermo, Italy, on 12-15 December 2000 and entered into force on 29 September 2003. The Convention is supplemented by three protocols: the "Protocol to Prevent, Suppress and Punish Trafficking in Persons, Especially Women and Children" (United Nations, 2000a); the "Protocol against the Smuggling of Migrants by Land, Sea and Air" (United Nations, 2000b); and the "Protocol against the Illicit Manufacturing of and Trafficking in Firearms, their Parts and Components and Ammunition". Countries have to be parties to the Convention before they can become parties to any of the Protocols. Some 80 countries signed the "Protocol to Prevent, Suppress and Punish Trafficking in Persons, Especially Women and Children" in Palermo on 12-15 December 2000. Currently there are 117 signatories and 169 parties to the Protocol.[3]

The "Protocol to Prevent, Suppress and Punish Trafficking in Persons, Especially Women and Children supplementing the United Nations Convention against Transnational Organized Crime" (the "UN Trafficking in Persons Protocol"), entered into force on 25 December 2003. The Protocol is the first global legally binding instrument with an agreed definition on trafficking in persons. According to Article 3(a) of the Protocol, "Trafficking in persons shall mean the recruitment, transportation, transfer, harbouring or receipt of persons, by means of the threat or use of force or other forms of coercion, of abduction, of fraud, of deception, of the abuse of power or of a position of vulnerability or of the giving or receiving of payments or benefits to achieve the consent of a person having control over another person, for the purpose of exploitation. Exploitation shall include, at a minimum, the exploitation of the prostitution of others or other forms of sexual exploitation, forced labour or services, slavery or practices similar to slavery, servitude or the removal of organs." The purpose of the Protocol is to protect and assist the victims of trafficking in persons with full respect for their human rights and to facilitate for the harmonisation of national approaches with regard to the establishment of domestic criminal offences that would support efficient international co-operation in investigating and prosecuting trafficking-in-persons cases.

Table 1.4. **Ratification of international and regional conventions on trafficking in persons and forced labour by OECD countries and APEC member economies**

	United Nations Protocol to Prevent, Suppress and Punish Trafficking in Persons, Especially Women and Children	United Nations Convention for the Suppression of the Traffic of Persons and of the Exploitation of the Prostitution of Others	Council of Europe Convention on Action against Trafficking in Human Beings	ILO Forced Labour Convention, 1930 (No. 29)	ILO Abolition of Forced Labour Convention, 1957 (No. 105)
Australia	R		n.a.	R	R
Austria	R		R	R	R
Belgium	R	AC	R	R	R
Brunei Darussalam			n.a.		
Canada	R		n.a.	R	R
Chile	R		n.a.	R	R
China, People's Republic of	AC		n.a.		
Czech Republic	R	D		R	R
Denmark	R	S	R	R	R
Estonia	R		R	R	R
Finland	A	R	R	R	R
France	R	AC	R	R	R
Germany	R		R	R	R
Greece	R		R	R	R
Hong Kong, China			n.a.	*	*
Hungary	R	AC	R	R	R
Iceland	R		R	R	R
Indonesia	R	S	n.a.	R	R
Ireland	R		R	R	R
Israel	R	AC	n.a.	R	R
Italy	R	AC	R	R	R
Japan	S	AC	n.a.	R	
Korea	S	AC	n.a.		
Luxembourg	R	R	R	R	R
Malaysia	AC		n.a.	R	
Mexico	R	AC	n.a.	R	R
Netherlands	A		R	R	R
New Zealand	R		n.a.	R	R
Norway	R	AC	R	R	R
Papua New Guinea			n.a.	R	R
Peru	R		n.a.	R	R
Philippines	R	R	n.a.	R	R
Poland	R	AC	R	R	R
Portugal	R	AC	R	R	R
Russian Federation	R	AC	n.a.	R	R
Singapore	AC	AC	n.a.	R	
Slovak Republic	R	D	R	R	R
Slovenia	R	D	R	R	R
Spain	R	AC	R	R	R
Sweden	R		R	R	R
Switzerland	R		R	R	R
Chinese Taipei	n.a.	n.a.	n.a.	n.a.	n.a.
Thailand	R		n.a.	R	R
Turkey	R		S	R	R
United Kingdom	R		R	R	R
United States	R		n.a.		R
Viet Nam	AC		n.a.	R	
Total					
S - Signature	2	2	1	0	0
R - Ratification	35	3	23	41	38
A - Acceptance	2	0	0	0	0
AP - Approval	0	0	0	0	0
AC - Accession	4	14	0	0	0
D - Succession	0	3	0	0	0
* - Notified as applicable	0	0	0	1	1

Notes: For UN Treaties, "Ratification" is defined as the international act whereby a state indicates its consent to be bound to a treaty if the parties intended to show their consent by such an act. In the case of bilateral treaties, ratification is usually accomplished by exchanging the requisite instruments, while in the case of multilateral treaties the usual procedure is for the depositary to collect the ratifications of all states, keeping all parties informed of the situation. The institution of ratification grants states the necessary timeframe to seek the required approval for the treaty on the domestic level and to enact the necessary legislation to give domestic effect to that treaty (Arts.2 (1) (b), 14 (1) and 16, Vienna Convention on the Law of Treaties 1969).

For UN Conventions, "Accession" is defined as the act whereby a state accepts the offer or the opportunity to become a party to a treaty already negotiated and signed by other states. It has the same legal effect as ratification. Accession usually occurs after the treaty has entered into force (Arts.2 (1) (b) and 15, Vienna Convention on the Law of Treaties 1969).

For ILO Conventions, ratifying countries commit themselves to applying the convention in national law and practice and reporting on its application at regular intervals.

The statistical data for Israel are supplied by and under the responsibility of the relevant Israeli authorities. The use of such data by the OECD is without prejudice to the status of the Golan Heights, East Jerusalem and Israeli settlements in the West Bank under the terms of international law.

Source: Based on the following information: United Nations (2000a), "Protocol to Prevent, Suppress and Punish Trafficking in Persons, Especially Women and Children, supplementing the United Nations Convention against Transnational Organized Crime", *Treaty Collection*, database, https://treaties.un.org/Pages/ViewDetails.aspx?src=IND&mtdsg_no=XVIII-12-a&chapter=18&lang=en; United Nations (1950), "Convention for the Suppression of the Traffic in Persons and of the Exploitation of the Prostitution of Others", *Treaty Collection*, database, https://treaties.un.org/Pages/ViewDetails.aspx?src=IND&mtdsg_no=VII-11-a&chapter=7&lang=en; Council of Europe (2008), "Status of Signature and Ratification of the Convention on Action against Trafficking in Human Beings", www.coe.int/t/dghl/monitoring/trafficking/Flags-sos_en.asp; ILO (1930a), "Ratifications of C029 – Forced Labour Convention, 1930 (No. 29)", www.ilo.org/dyn/normlex/en/f?p=1000:11300:0::NO:11300:P11300_INSTRUMENT_ID:312174; ILO (1957a), "Ratifications of C105 – Abolition of Forced Labour Convention, 1957 (No. 105)", www.ilo.org/dyn/normlex/en/f?p=1000:11300:0::NO:11300:P11300_INSTRUMENT_ID:312250.

The United Nations Convention for the Suppression of the Traffic in Persons and of the Exploitation of the Prostitution of Others

The "Convention for the Suppression of the Traffic in Persons and of the Exploitation of the Prostitution of Others" (United Nations, 1950) was approved by the General Assembly in 1949 and entered into force on 25 July 1951. Although "trafficking" is not explicitly defined in the Convention, Article 1 sets out that Parties to the Convention should punish "any person who, to gratify the passions of another: 1) procures, entices or leads away, for purposes of prostitution, another person, even with the consent of that person; 2) exploits the prostitution of another person, even with the consent of that person." State Parties to the Convention should also punish anyone who "keeps or manages, or knowingly finances or takes part in the financing of a brothel" or "knowingly lets or rents a building or other place or any part thereof for the purpose of the prostitution of others."

The Universal Declaration of Human Rights

The "Universal Declaration of Human Rights" was adopted by the UN General Assembly on 10 December 1948 (United Nations, 1948). The "Universal Declaration of Human Rights" establishes in Article 4 that "No one shall be held in slavery or servitude; slavery and the slave trade shall be prohibited in all their forms" and that everyone has the right to the free choice of employment (Article 23[1]).

ILO Forced Labour Convention

Adopted by the International Labour Conference at its 14th session (June 1930), the ILO (1930b) "Forced Labour Convention" was the first international legal instrument providing a definition of forced and compulsory labour and listing possible exceptions. Forced or compulsory labour is defined as "all work or service which is exacted from any person under the menace of any penalty and for which the said person has not offered himself voluntarily." In June 2014, the ILO International Labour Conference voted to adopt a Protocol and a Recommendation which supplement the Forced Labour

Convention, 1930 (No. 29), in order to provide guidance on effective measures to be taken regarding prevention, protection and remedy to eliminate all forms of forced labour.

ILO Abolition of Forced Labour Convention

After the Second World War, the ILO adopted new approaches to forced labour. The ILO (1957b) "Abolition of Forced Labour Convention" was adopted by the International Labour Conference at its 40th session (June 1957) and supplements the provision of Convention No. 29 on Forced Labour. Article 1 reads that "Member of the International Labour Organisation which ratifies this Convention undertakes to suppress and not to make use of any form of forced or compulsory labour (a) as a means of political coercion or education or as a punishment for holding or expressing political views or views ideologically opposed to the established political, social or economic system; (b) as a method of mobilising and using labour for purposes of economic development; (c) as a means of labour discipline; (d) as a punishment for having participated in strikes; (e) as a means of racial, social, national or religious discrimination."

Inter-American Convention on International Traffic in Minors

The "Inter-American Convention on International Traffic in Minors" was adopted in 1994 and entered into force in 1997. The Convention is a regional treaty that aims to ensure the protection of minors against trafficking. The Convention defines international traffic in minors as "the abduction, removal or retention, or attempted abduction, removal or retention, of a minor for unlawful purposes or by unlawful means." State parties under the Convention should institute a system of mutual legal assistance dedicated to the prevention and punishment of the international traffic in minors, as well as adopt related administrative and legal provisions to that effect. Although the Convention contains few specific provisions on prevention or protection of victims of trafficking, it requires State parties to protect minors in consideration of their best interests (Article 1a) and "ensure the prompt return of minors who are victims of international traffic to the State of their habitual residence, bearing in mind the best interests of the minors" (Article 1c).

South Asian Association for Regional Cooperation (SAARC) Convention on Preventing and Combating Trafficking in Women and Children for Prostitution

Adopted in 2002, the purpose of the "SAARC Convention on Preventing and Combating Trafficking in Women and Children for Prostitution" (SAARC, 2002) is to promote co-operation amongst SAARC Member States so that they may effectively deal with the various aspects of prevention, interdiction and suppression of trafficking in women and children as well as the repatriation and rehabilitation of victims of trafficking and prevent the use of women and children in international prostitution networks. Article 1.3 of the Convention defines trafficking as the moving, selling or buying of women and children for prostitution within and outside a country for monetary or other considerations with or without the consent of the person subjected to trafficking. A persons subjected to trafficking is defined as women and children victimised or forced into prostitution by the traffickers by deception, threat, coercion, kidnapping, sale, fraudulent marriage, child marriage, or any other unlawful means.

Article VIII(1) established that State Parties to the Convention shall provide sufficient means, training and assistance to their respective authorities to enable them to effectively conduct inquiries, investigations and prosecution of trafficking offences. In addition to this, the SAARC Convention includes a number of provisions that address the prevention of trafficking and protection of victims. Article VIII(8) establishes that State parties shall "promote awareness, *inter alia*, through the use of the media, of the problem of trafficking in Women and Children and its underlying causes including the projection of negative images of women." Article IX(2) and (3) state that State Parties shall establish protective homes or shelters for rehabilitation of victims of trafficking and provide legal advice, counselling, job training and health care facilities for the victims. Also, for victims of cross-border trafficking that are waiting for the completion of arrangements for their repatriation, State Parties shall make suitable provisions for their care and maintenance and shall provide legal advice and health care facilities.

Association of Southeast Asian Nations (ASEAN) Declaration Against Trafficking in Persons Particularly Women and Children

The "ASEAN Declaration Against Trafficking in Persons Particularly Women and Children" (2004) was adopted on 29 November 2004 during the 10th Summit of the Association of Southeast Asian Nations (ASEAN) by the ten ASEAN heads of state. The purpose of the declaration is to establish a regional focal network for sharing of information, views, and strengthen operations and co-operation to prevent and combat trafficking in persons, particularly women and children, in the ASEAN region. Further demonstrating their commitment to combatting trafficking in persons, ASEAN heads of state signed the legally binding ASEAN (2015) "Convention Against Trafficking in Persons, Especially Women and Children" on 21 November 2015.

The Coordinated Mekong Ministerial Initiative Against Trafficking (COMMIT)

In 2004, Cambodia, China, Lao PDR, Myanmar, Thailand, and Viet Nam signed a Memorandum of Understanding (MOU) on Cooperation against Trafficking in Persons at the Ministerial level. The MOU commits the governments to a human-trafficking response that meets international standards, and highlights the need for multi-lateral, bilateral, and government-NGO co-operation in the fight against human trafficking. At the national level, the COMMIT Process is governed by the six national COMMIT Taskforces that are each comprised of government officials from the relevant ministries – including police, justice, social welfare, and women's affairs. At the regional level, two representatives from each COMMIT Taskforce meet at least twice a year with the goal of setting priorities and holding discussions on urgent issues at a regional level.

Council of Europe Convention on Action Against Trafficking in Human Beings (European Trafficking Convention)

The Council of Europe "Convention on Action Against Trafficking in Human Beings" was adopted on 16 May 2005 and entered into force on 1 February 2008. The convention focuses on the protection of victims of trafficking and their rights, as well as the prevention of trafficking and prosecution of traffickers, and uses the same definition of trafficking in human beings as the UN Trafficking in Persons Protocol definition.

EU Directive 2011/36/EU of 5 April 2011 (EU Trafficking Directive)

The "EU Directive 2011/36/EU of the European Parliament and of the Council of 5 April 2011 on preventing and combating trafficking in human beings and protecting its victims" (European Union, 2011) uses the UN Trafficking in Persons Protocol definition of trafficking in persons for the definition of trafficking in human beings. The EU Directive requires Member States to criminalise all forms of trafficking and to assign penalties for trafficking offences. According to Article 9(1), Member States shall ensure that investigation into or prosecution of trafficking offences is "not dependent on reporting or accusation by a victim and that criminal proceedings may continue even if the victim has withdrawn his or her statement."

The establishment of an EU Anti-Trafficking Coordinator was originally discussed in the Stockholm Programme, but later elaborated on in the EU Trafficking Directive. In addition to improving co-ordination and coherence among EU institutions, EU agencies, Member States and international actors and developing existing and new EU policies to address trafficking in persons, the Coordinator is responsible for overseeing the implementation of the EU Strategy towards the Eradication of Trafficking in Human Beings 2012–16 (European Commission, 2012). The Strategy identifies five priorities that the European Union should focus on in order to address the issue of trafficking in human beings and outlines a number of proposed actions implement over the next five years together with other actors (e.g. Member States, third countries, international organisations, civil society and the private sector). The priorities and corresponding actions are (European Commission, 2012):

A. Identifying, protecting and assisting victims of trafficking
   - Action 1: Establishment of national and transnational referral mechanisms
   - Action 2: Identification of victims
   - Action 3: Protection of child victims of trafficking
   - Action 4: Provision of information on the rights of victims

B. Stepping up the prevention of trafficking in human beings
   - Action 1: Understanding and reducing demand
   - Action 2: Promote the establishment of a private sector platform
   - Action 3: EU-wide awareness raising activities and prevention programmes

C. Increased prosecution of traffickers
   - Action 1: Establishment of national multidisciplinary law enforcement units
   - Action 2: Ensuring proactive financial investigation
   - Action 3: Increasing cross-border police and judicial co-operation
   - Action 4: Increasing co-operation beyond borders

D. Enhanced co-ordination and co-operation among key actors and policy coherence
   - Action 1: Strengthening the EU Network of National Rapporteurs or equivalent mechanisms
   - Action 2: Co-ordinating EU external policy activities
   - Action 3: Promoting the establishment of a civil society platform
   - Action 4: Reviewing projects funded by the EU
   - Action 5: Strengthen the fundamental rights in anti-trafficking policy and related actions
   - Action 6: Co-ordinating training needs in a multidisciplinary context

E. Increased knowledge of and effective response to emerging concerns related to all forms of trafficking in human beings
   - Action 1: Developing an EU-wide system for data collection
   - Action 2: Developing knowledge relating to the gender dimension of trafficking and vulnerable groups
   - Action 3: Understanding online recruitment
   - Action 4: Targeting trafficking for labour exploitation

OSCE Ministerial Council Decision No. 2/03 on Combating Trafficking in Human Beings

Similar to the EU Trafficking Directive, the OSCE (Organization for Security and Co-operation in Europe) "Decision No. 2/03 on Combatting Trafficking in Human Beings", which was adopted in December 2003 is based on the UN Trafficking in Persons Protocol definition of trafficking in persons. The OSCE "Action Plan to Combat Trafficking in Human Beings" intends to provide participating States with a comprehensive toolkit to help them implement their commitments to combating trafficking in persons. It provides participating States with follow-up mechanisms such as Human Dimension Implementation Meetings and Review Conferences, which promote co-ordination between individual participating States, but also recommends States to, for example, consider appointing national rapporteurs or other mechanisms for monitoring the anti-trafficking activities, and establishing anti-trafficking commissions (taskforces) or similar bodies responsible for co-ordinating activities within a country among State agencies and NGOs. It covers the protection of victims, the prevention of trafficking in persons and the prosecution of those who facilitate or commit the crime. The Action Plan provides recommendations as to how participating States may best deal with political, economic, legal, law enforcement, educational and other aspects of the problem.

US Victims of Trafficking and Violence Protection Act

The US "Victims of Trafficking and Violence Protection Act" (TVPA) of 2000, the "Trafficking Victims Protection Reauthorization Act" of 2003, the "Trafficking Victims Protection Reauthorization Act" of 2005, the "Trafficking Victims Protection Reauthorization Act" of 2008, and the "Trafficking Victims Protection Reauthorization Act" of 2013 provide tools to combat trafficking in persons both worldwide and domestically in the United States. Section 103(8) of the Act defines severe forms of trafficking in persons as 1) sex trafficking in which a commercial sex act is induced by force, fraud, or coercion, or in which the person induced to perform such act has not attained 18 years of age; or 2) the recruitment, harbouring, transportation, provision, or obtaining of a person for labour or services, through the use of force, fraud, or coercion for the purpose of subjection to involuntary servitude, peonage, debt bondage, or slavery. The TVPA provides the basis for an annual report on trafficking in persons and establishes an inter-agency taskforce to co-ordinate federal anti-trafficking action. The TVPA allows trafficking victims to benefit from residence and work authorisation under certain circumstances.

US Agency for International Development (USAID) Counter-Trafficking in Persons Policy and Agency-Wide Counter Trafficking in Persons Code of Conduct

Being among the largest donors engaged in counter-trafficking in persons, USAID has implemented a "Counter-Trafficking in Persons Policy" and an "Agency-Wide Counter Trafficking in Persons Code of Conduct" that both incorporate the principles set out in the TVPA.

The Policy is built on 4Ps: Prevention; Protection for victims; Prosecution of traffickers; and Partnership and co-ordination of stakeholders. The Policy sets out five programming objectives for the Agency relating to counter-trafficking in persons (USAID, 2012):

1. efforts to combat TIP integrated into relevant Agency initiatives and programmes
2. improved codification and application of learning in efforts to combat TIP
3. enhanced institutional accountability to combat TIP as a result of training and co-ordination
4. augmented C-TIP investments in critical TIP challenge countries
5. increased investments in TIP prevention and protection in conflict and crisis-affected areas.

Through the Code of Conduct, USAID pledges to: 1) prohibit USAID contractors, subcontractors, grantees and sub grantees during the period of performance of their contracts or awards from engaging in trafficking in persons, procuring commercial sex acts, or using forced labour; 2) sensitise USAID personnel to human trafficking and the ethical conduct requirements that prohibit the procurement of commercial sex and the use of trafficked labour; 3) equip USAID personnel with the necessary knowledge and tools to recognise, report, and address human-trafficking offenses; 4) require USAID personnel to report suspected cases of USAID employee misconduct as well as waste, fraud, and abuse in USAID programmes as related to human trafficking; and 5) designate a Counter Trafficking in Persons Co-ordinator at all Missions to serve as the primary point of contact for this issue. The Co-ordinator will disseminate information, respond to inquiries, and liaise with appropriate staff in developing anti-human trafficking strategies.

Mexican General Act for Prevention, Punishment and Eradication of Crimes in Trafficking in Persons and for the Protection and Assistance of Victims of this Crime

In Mexico, the "General Act for Prevention, Punishment and Eradication of Crimes in Trafficking in Persons and for the Protection and Assistance of Victims of this Crime" (*Ley General para Prevenir, Sancionar y Erradicar los Delitos en Materia de Trata de Personas y para la Protección y Asistencia a las Víctimas de Estos Delitos*) came into force on 14 June 2012 (Cámara de Diputados, 2012). It determines the co-ordination of federal, state and municipal actors involved in the prevention and prosecution of trafficking in persons, as well as the protection of victims. It sets out the criminal actions and corresponding penalties for crimes of trafficking in persons, and establishes a number of mechanisms to effectively protect the life, dignity, freedom, integrity and safety of persons from offences set out in the Act. The Act does not only make the trafficking of persons a criminal offence but also criminalises slavery, debt bondage, the imposition of forced labour or services, and the exploitation of labour.

The "National Programme for the Prevention and Punishment of Trafficking in Persons 2010-12" (*Programa Nacional para Prevenir y Sancionar la Trata de Personas 2010-12*) (*Secretaría de Relaciones Exteriores*, 2011) was drawn up by an Inter-Ministerial Committee set up to prevent and penalise the trafficking of persons and was adopted on 6 January 2011. The Programme has four objectives: increasing knowledge of trafficking in persons; preventing and raising awareness of trafficking in persons;

contributing to the effective functioning of the justice system; and providing comprehensive protection for victims.

A Special Prosecutor for Crimes of Violence against Women and Trafficking (*La Fiscalía Especial para los Delitos de Violencia contra las Mujeres y Trata de Personas*, FEVIMTRA) attached to the Office for Human Rights, Victim and Community Services of the Attorney General's Office (PGR), is responsible for investigating and prosecuting federal crimes related to violence against women and trafficking in persons, and to contribute to citizens' right to obtain justice.

New Zealand Plan of Action to Prevent People Trafficking

In New Zealand, the "Plan of Action to Prevent People Trafficking" (NZ Department of Labour, 2009) was co-ordinated by the Department of Labour on behalf of an Interagency Working Group on People Trafficking comprised of the Departments of Labour and Prime Minister and Cabinet; the Ministries of Justice, Foreign Affairs and Trade, Health, Social Development, and Women's Affairs; and the New Zealand Police and Customs Service. The Plan of Action sets out ten principles that focus on the prevention, and prosecution of trafficking, and protection of victims of trafficking. This includes training for officials to identify trafficking, assistance, health services, housing and protection for trafficking victims, and compensation for victims. The Plan of Action mainstreams human trafficking prevention and assistance into existing government initiatives and programmes.

Private sector initiatives

The private sector has a key role to play in the prevention of trafficking in persons as traffickers cannot operate on a large scale without legitimate businesses. Examples highlighted by BEST (Businesses Ending Slavery and Trafficking) are: traffickers advertising their victims on websites and taking them to hotels for sexual exploitation; traffickers using airlines and ports to transport victims; and traffickers using banks for their financial transactions (BEST, Washington Engage and End Human Trafficking Now, n.d.). Also, due to a lack of awareness or a lack of anti-trafficking protocols, employees of legitimate business have difficulties recognising or preventing trafficking in persons, or do not know how to respond when recognised. As outlined below, there are a number of private sector initiatives that aim to address these issues. Less common are government anti-trafficking measures aimed at the private sector (e.g. the "California Transparency in Supply Chains Act" of 2010).

Athens Ethical Principles

Companies are increasingly integrating corporate social responsibility considerations into their business models. A prominent example of a private sector initiative to combat trafficking in persons is the End Human Trafficking Now (EHTN) association. EHTN is an association created by the business community that during the Round Table of the Business Community Against the Trafficking of Human Beings on 23 January 2006 adopted the "Athens Ethical Principles" (EHTN, 2006). The purpose of the Principles is to combat human trafficking worldwide through the focus of seven main areas:

1. Demonstrate the position of zero tolerance towards trafficking in human beings, especially women and children for sexual exploitation (Policy Setting).

2. Contribute to prevention of trafficking in human beings including awareness-raising campaigns and education (Public Awareness-Raising).
3. Develop a corporate strategy for an anti-trafficking policy which will permeate all activities (Strategic Planning).
4. Ensure that personnel fully comply with the anti-trafficking policy (Personnel Policy Enforcement).
5. Encourage business partners, including suppliers, to apply ethical principles against human trafficking (Supply Chain Tracing).
6. In an effort to increase enforcement, it is necessary to call on governments to initiate a process of revision of laws and regulations that are directly or indirectly related to enhancing anti-trafficking policies (Government Advocacy).
7. Report and share information on best practices (Transparency).

In addition to benefitting society at large, the focus on combatting human trafficking is also beneficial for the business community (Box 1.1).

Box 1.1. **Benefits to the business community in focussing on combatting human trafficking**

"As an illegitimate form of business, it negatively impacts the functioning of the legitimate business sector and puts the development of sound economic systems into danger. It is a ground where corruptive practices and money laundering proliferate. Potential risks for companies being associated with human trafficking include legal litigations, financial and brand damages. Since loss of reputation is a disaster for any company, it is their vital interest to pay attention to these risks and exercise due diligence to eliminate or minimise them.

An active stance against human trafficking enhances brand value and attracts consumers interested in ethical brand. Experience shows that work for an ethical brand makes employees proud and happy which means higher retention rate and increased profit for a company. Additional gains include strengthening of business partnerships, ensuring market access and attracting new business opportunities. Corporations are increasingly requesting from their suppliers commitment to ethical business practice, including with respect to human trafficking and labor exploitation. A zero-tolerance policy, advocacy and engagement earn business a leadership position in their industry and community, build trust and good working relationships with local communities, and guarantee the highest distinction of its corporate image."

Source: End Human Trafficking Now. (n.d.). *Background*, www.endhumantraffickingnow.com/background/.

The Luxor Implementation Guidelines

The "Luxor Implementation Guidelines to the Athens Ethical Principles" (EHTN, 2010) was one of the main outcomes of the Luxor International Forum in 2010. The Guidelines follow the structure of the "Athens Ethical Principles" and present a number of actions within each area that companies must take.

UN.GIFT (UN Global Initiative to Fight Human Trafficking) and End Human Trafficking Now (2010) also launched a modular "Human Trafficking and Business eLearning Programme" for business leaders, managers and employees of business companies that was developed together with Microsoft. The aim of the course is to educate them on what human trafficking is, identify where it might be a risk to their business and point to actions they can take to address this risk.

International Code of Conduct for Private Security Service Providers

The "International Code of Conduct for Private Security Providers" (ICoC) is a multi-stakeholder initiative convened by the Swiss Bureau of Diplomatic Security, the Bureau of Democracy, Human Rights and Labour, and the Department of Defence. Companies that sign the code make the commitment that they "will not, and will require their Personnel not to, engage in trafficking in persons. Signatory Companies will, and will require their Personnel to, remain vigilant for all instances of trafficking in persons and, where discovered, report such instances to Competent Authorities" (International Code of Conduct Association, 2010, para. 39).

Washington BEST Code of Conduct and Principles for Implementation

The "Washington BEST Code of Conduct and Principles for Implementation" is a tool for small and medium-sized enterprises to prevent trafficking in persons within their operations and business-to-business networks. It is a partnership between Businesses Ending Slavery and Trafficking (BEST), Washington Engage and End Human Trafficking Now. By signing the Principles, companies commit to:

1. comply with applicable laws and regulations
2. assess trafficking-related risks and impacts
3. implement an anti-trafficking management system with protocols to prevent, report, and remedy incidents
4. align existing policies with the anti-trafficking policy
5. provide notice of the anti-trafficking policy to employees and business partners including suppliers, contractors, and sub-contractors
6. train employees to comply with the anti-trafficking policy and protocols
7. report and share best practices.

California Transparency in Supply Chains Act of 2010

The "California Transparency in Supply Chains Act of 2010" (State of California, 2010) requires retail sellers and manufacturers doing business in the State of California and that have annual worldwide gross receipts that exceed USD 100 million to disclose their efforts to eradicate slavery and trafficking in persons from their direct supply chains for tangible goods offered for sale. The reasoning behind the Act is that this will contribute to educating consumers on how to purchase goods that are produced by companies that responsibly manage their supply chains. Section 2(i) of the Act states that "Absent publicly available disclosures, consumers are at a disadvantage in being able to distinguish companies on the merits of their efforts to supply products free from the taint of slavery and trafficking. Consumers are at a disadvantage in being able to force the eradication of slavery and trafficking by way of their purchasing decisions." The retail seller or manufacturer should disclose, at a minimum, to what extent it does each of the following:

1. Engages in verification of product supply chains to evaluate and address risks of human trafficking and slavery. The disclosure shall specify if the verification was not conducted by a third party.
2. Conducts audits of suppliers to evaluate supplier compliance with company standards for trafficking and slavery in supply chains. The disclosure shall specify if the verification was not an independent, unannounced audit.
3. Requires direct suppliers to certify that materials incorporated into the product comply with the laws regarding slavery and human trafficking of the country or countries in which they are doing business.
4. Maintains internal accountability standards and procedures for employees or contractors failing to meet company standards regarding slavery and trafficking.
5. Provides company employees and management, who have direct responsibility for supply chain management, training on human trafficking and slavery, particularly with respect to mitigating risks within the supply chains of products.

Notes

1. According to Article 3(a) of the United Nations "Protocol to Prevent, Suppress and Punish Trafficking in Persons, Especially Women and Children" (the "UN Trafficking in Persons Protocol"), "Trafficking in persons shall mean the recruitment, transportation, transfer, harbouring or receipt of persons, by means of the threat or use of force or other forms of coercion, of abduction, of fraud, of deception, of the abuse of power or of a position of vulnerability or of the giving or receiving of payments or benefits to achieve the consent of a person having control over another person, for the purpose of exploitation. Exploitation shall include, at a minimum, the exploitation of the prostitution of others or other forms of sexual exploitation, forced labour or services, slavery or practices similar to slavery, servitude or the removal of organs."
2. The ILO defines forced or compulsory labour as "all work or service which is exacted from any person under the menace of any penalty and for which the said person has not offered himself voluntarily" (Article 2.1 of the Forced Labour Convention, 1930 [No. 29]).
3. As of 11 February 2016.

References

Arlacchi, A. (2000), "Opening statement of Pino Arlacchi, Under-Secretary-General Director-General to the International Seminar on Trafficking in Human Beings", Brasilia, 28-29 November 2000, www.unodc.org/unodc/en/aboutunodc/speeches/speech_2000-11-28_1.html.

ASEAN (Association of Southeast Asian Nations) (2015), "ASEAN Convention Against Trafficking in Persons, Especially Women and Children", Kuala Lumpur, 21 November 2015, www.asean.org/storage/images/2015/November/actip/ACTIP.PDF.

ASEAN (2004), "ASEAN Declaration Against Trafficking in Persons Particularly Women and Children", Vientiane, 29 November, www1.umn.edu/humanrts/research/Philippines/ASEAN%20Declaration%20Against%20Trafficking%20in%20Persons%20Particularly%20Women%20and%20Children.pdf.

BEST (Businesses Ending Slavery and Trafficking), Washington Engage and End Human Trafficking Now (n.d.), "Washington Best Principles", www.bestalliance.org/uploads/5/0/0/4/50047795/best-intro.principles.guidelines.11.pdf.

Cámara de Diputados (2012), "Ley General para Prevenir, Sancionar y Erradicar los Delitos en Materia de Trata de Personas y para la Protección y Asistencia a las Víctimas de Estos Delitos", Government of Mexico, www.diputados.gob.mx/LeyesBiblio/pdf/LGPSEDMTP.pdf.

Council of Europe (2008), "Status of Signature and Ratification of the Convention on Action against Trafficking in Human Beings", *Council of Europe Treaty Series*, www.coe.int/t/dghl/monitoring/trafficking/Flags-sos_en.asp.

Council of Europe (2005), "Convention on Action against Trafficking in Human Beings and its Explanatory Report", *Council of Europe Treaty Series*, No. 197, Warsaw, 16 May, www.coe.int/t/dghl/monitoring/trafficking/Source/PDF_Conv_197_Trafficking_Erev.pdf.

EHTN (End Human Trafficking Now) (2010), "Luxor Implementation Guidelines to the Athens Ethical Principles", www.unglobalcompact.org/docs/issues_doc/human_rights/Resources/Luxor_Implementation_Guidelines_Ethical_Principles.pdf.

EHTN (2006), "Athens Ethical Principles", www.ungift.org/docs/ungift/pdf/Athens_principles.pdf.

EHTN (n.d.), *Background*, www.endhumantraffickingnow.com/background/.

European Commission (2012), "Communication from the Commission to the European Parliament, the Council, the European Economic and Social Committee and the Committee of the Regions: The EU Strategy towards the Eradication of Trafficking in Human Beings 2012–16", COM(2012) 286final, Brussels, 19 June, http://eur-lex.europa.eu/LexUriServ/LexUriServ.do?uri=COM:2012:0286:FIN:EN:PDF.

European Union (2011), "Directive 2011/36/EU of the European Parliament and of the Council of 5 April 2011 on preventing and combating trafficking in human beings and protecting its victims, and replacing Council Framework Decision 2002/629/JHA", *Official Journal of the European Union*, Strasbourg, 5 April, http://eur-lex.europa.eu/LexUriServ/LexUriServ.do?uri=OJ:L:2011:101:0001:0011:EN:PDF.

Eurostat (2015), *Trafficking in Human Beings: 2015 edition*, Publications Office of the European Union, Luxembourg.

GTZ (*Gesellschaft für Technische Zusammenarbeit*) (2008), *Trafficking in Persons as a Human Rights Issue* GTZ, Eschborn, www.oecd.org/dac/gender-development/44896390.pdf.

Governments of the Kingdom of Cambodia, the People's Republic of China, the Lao People's Democratic Republic, the Union of Myanmar, the Kingdom of Thailand and the Socialist Republic of Vietnam (2004), "Memorandum of Understanding on Cooperation against Trafficking in Persons in the Greater Mekong Sub-Region", Yangon, 29 October, www.no-trafficking.org/reports_docs/commit/commit_eng_mou.pdf.

Haken, J. (2011), *Transnational Crime in The Developing World*, Global Financial Integrity, Washington, DC, p. 56, www.gfintegrity.org/storage/gfip/documents/reports/transcrime/gfi_transnational_crime_web.pdf.

ILO (International Labour Organization) (2015), *Profits and Poverty: The Economics of Forced Labour*, ILO, Geneva.

ILO (2012), *ILO 2012 Global Estimate of Forced Labour: Results and Methodology*, ILO, Geneva.

ILO (1957a), "Ratifications of C105 - Abolition of Forced Labour Convention, 1957 (No. 105)", www.ilo.org/dyn/normlex/en/f?p=1000:11300:0::NO:11300:P11300_INSTRUMENT_ID:312250.

ILO (1957b), "Abolition of Forced Labour Convention, 1957 (No. 105)", ILO, Geneva, 25 June, www.ilo.org/dyn/normlex/en/f?p=1000:12100:0::NO::P12100_ILO_CODE:C105.

ILO (1930a), "Ratifications of C029 - Forced Labour Convention, 1930 (No. 29)", www.ilo.org/dyn/normlex/en/f?p=1000:11300:0::NO:11300:P11300_INSTRUMENT_ID:312174.

ILO (1930b), "Forced Labour Convention, 1930 (No. 29)", Geneva, 28 June, www.ilo.org/dyn/normlex/en/f?p=NORMLEXPUB:12100:0::NO::P12100_INSTRUMENT_ID:312174.

International Code of Conduct Association (2010), "International Code of Conduct for Private Sector Security Service Providers", http://icoca.ch/en/the_icoc.

Luna, D. M. (2012), "The destructive impact of illicit trade and the illegal economy on economic growth, sustainable development, and global security", statement, OECD High-Level Risk Forum, Paris, 26 October 2012.

NZ Department of Labour. (2009), "Plan of Action to Prevent People Trafficking", Department of Labour, Wellington, New Zealand, www.dol.govt.nz/publications/research/people-trafficking/people-trafficking.pdf.

Organization for Security and Co-operation in Europe (2003), "Decision No. 2/03: Combating Trafficking in Human Beings", MC(11) Journal No. 2, Agenda item 8, Maastricht, 2 December, www.osce.org/odihr/23866?download=true.

Organization of American States (1994), "Inter-American Convention on International Traffic in Minors (B-57)", *Multilateral Treaties*, Department of International Law, Mexico, D.F., Mexico, 18 March, www.oas.org/dil/treaties_B-57_Inter-American_Convention_on_International_Traffic_in_Minors.htm.

Secretaría de Relaciones Exteriores (2011), "Programa Nacional para Prevenir y Sancionar la Trata de Personas 2010-12", *Boletín Informativo, 209*, 14 January, http://scm.oas.org/pdfs/2011/CP25564S-3.pdf.

Shelley, L. (2010), "Restoring trust for peace and security", 14th International Anti-Corruption Conference, Bangkok, Thailand, 10-13 November, http://14iacc.org/wp-content/uploads/LouiseShelleypeaceandsecurity14IACC.pdf.

SAARC (South Asian Association for Regional Cooperation) (2002), "SAARC Convention on Preventing and Combating Trafficking in Women and Children for Prostitution", Kathmandu, 5 January, http://no-trafficking.org/content/pdf/saarc_convention.pdf.

State of California (2010), "California Transparency in Supply Chains Act of 2010", SB 657, www.state.gov/documents/organization/164934.pdf.

UN.GIFT (UN Global Initiative to Fight Human Trafficking) and End Human Trafficking Now (2010), "Launch of the E-learning tool", End Human Trafficking Now: Enforcing the UN Protocol, The Luxor International Forum, Egypt, 10-12 December 2010, www.ungift.org/doc/knowledgehub/events/Luxor_eLearning_Tool.pdf.

United Nations (2000a), "Protocol to Prevent, Suppress and Punish Trafficking in Persons, Especially Women and Children, supplementing the United Nations Convention against Transnational Organized Crime", *Treaty Collection*, database, https://treaties.un.org/Pages/ViewDetails.aspx?src=IND&mtdsg_no=XVIII-12-a&chapter=18&lang=en.

United Nations (2000b), "Protocol against the Smuggling of Migrants by Land, Sea and Air, supplementing the United Nations Convention against Transnational Organized Crime", *United Nations Treaty Series*, vol. 2241, No. 39574, New York, 15 November, p. 507, https://treaties.un.org/doc/Publication/UNTS/Volume%202241/v2241.pdf.

United Nations (1950), "Convention for the Suppression of the Traffic in Persons and of the Exploitation of the Prostitution of Others", *Treaty Collection*, database, Lake Success, New York, 21 March, https://treaties.un.org/Pages/ViewDetails.aspx?src=IND&mtdsg_no=VII-11-a&chapter=7&lang=en.

United Nations (1948), "Universal Declaration of Human Rights", General Assembly Resolution 217 A, A/RES/3/217 A, Paris, 10 December, www.un-documents.net/a3r217a.htm.

UNODC (United Nations Office on Drugs and Crime) (2014), *Global Report on Trafficking in Persons 2014*, United Nations, New York, www.unodc.org/documents/data-and-analysis/glotip/GLOTIP_2014_full_report.pdf.

UNODC (2012), *Global Report on Trafficking in Persons 2012,* United Nations, New York, www.unodc.org/unodc/en/data-and-analysis/glotip_2012.html.

USAID (United States Agency for International Development) (2012), "USAID Counter-Trafficking in Persons Policy February 2012", USDAID, Washington, DC, http://pdf.usaid.gov/pdf_docs/PDACT111.pdf.

USAID (2011), "Guidance on the Implementation of Agency-Wide Counter Trafficking in Persons Code of Conduct", http://pdf.usaid.gov/pdf_docs/PDACT175.pdf.

US Department of State (2015), *Trafficking in Persons Report July 2015*, US Department of State, Washington, DC.

US Department of State (2013), "Trafficking Victims Protection Reauthorization Act of 2013", Title XII of the Violence Against Women Reauthorization Act of 2013, Pub. L. 113-4, 127 STAT. 54, www.gpo.gov/fdsys/pkg/PLAW-113publ4/html/PLAW-113publ4.htm.

US Department of State (2008), "William Wilberforce Trafficking Victims Protection Reauthorization Act of 2008", Pub. L. No. 110-457, 122 STAT. 5044, www.state.gov/j/tip/laws/113178.htm.

US Department of State (2005), "Trafficking Victims Protection Reauthorization Act of 2005", Pub. L. No. 109–164, 119 STAT. 3558, www.state.gov/j/tip/laws/61106.htm.

US Department of State (2003), "Trafficking Victims Protection Reauthorization Act of 2003", Pub. L. No. 108–193, 117 STAT. 2875, www.state.gov/j/tip/laws/61130.htm.

US Department of State (2000), "Victims of Trafficking and Violence Protection Act of 2000", Pub. L. No. 106–386, 114 STAT. 1464, www.state.gov/j/tip/laws/61124.htm.

Chapter 2

Trafficking in persons and corruption: A symbiotic relationship

Trafficking in persons could not occur at the large scale that it currently does without the leverage supplied by corruption. This chapter explores this link between trafficking in persons and corruption, focusing on who the corrupt actors are, the types of corrupt acts they commit, and where in the trafficking chain corruption takes place.

Corruption facilitates the illegal economy just as transparency and the rule of law enable legal markets. Organised trafficking simply cannot take place without corruption. It has been argued that trafficking in persons would not be as prevalent and widespread if it were not for the leverage supplied by corruption (Tremblay, 2010). Similarly, it has been noted that human trafficking could not occur on the scale it does if it were not for the complicity and collusion of corrupt officials with criminal gangs (Holmes, 2009).

The aim of corruption in the trafficking in persons cycle is said to have four main goals (IACC, 2010):

1. to allow the crime to be invisible
2. to facilitate the impunity once a case of trafficking in persons is detected
3. to facilitate the execution of the crime
4. to assure the re-victimisation of the trafficked victims.

Corrupt law enforcement agents facilitate the recruitment, transportation and exploitation of trafficking victims, and corrupt criminal justice authorities can help traffickers by obstructing investigations and prosecutions of cases as well as hinder the protection of victims of trafficking. Corrupt officials play an important role in the different stages of the trafficking-in-persons supply chain. Obtaining fraudulent invitations or forged documents may be facilitated by corrupt officials at the recruitment stage. At the transportation stage, officials may turn a blind eye and ignore victims of trafficking – allowing them to cross borders – in exchange for bribes. At the exploitation phase, they may practice extortion (UNODC, 2008). Corruption involving the private sector – for example overseas employment agencies, travel agencies, model agencies, marriage bureaus, and hotels – may also contribute to trafficking in persons (UNODC, 2011).

Since corruption is central to the success of traffickers, corruption becomes a necessary investment for criminals. Studies suggest that corruption is one of the most important cost factors for traffickers (PACO, 2002). Corruption allows for the massive enrichment of traffickers and helps to lure individuals from the public and private sector into trafficking networks – either by joining the networks or facilitating their operations.

Countries that make the least effort to fight trafficking in persons are also those who tend to have high levels of perceived corruption. Figure 2.1 compares the categorisation of countries in the US *Trafficking in Persons 2014* report to the ranking of countries in Transparency International's *2014 Corruption Perception Index*. Countries with the highest perception of corruption are found in the category "Tier 3", which represents countries whose governments do not fully comply with the minimum standards set out in the US "Trafficking Victims Protection Act" and are not making significant efforts to do so.

Figure 2.1. **Countries that make the least effort to fight trafficking in persons are also those who tend to have high levels of perceived corruption**

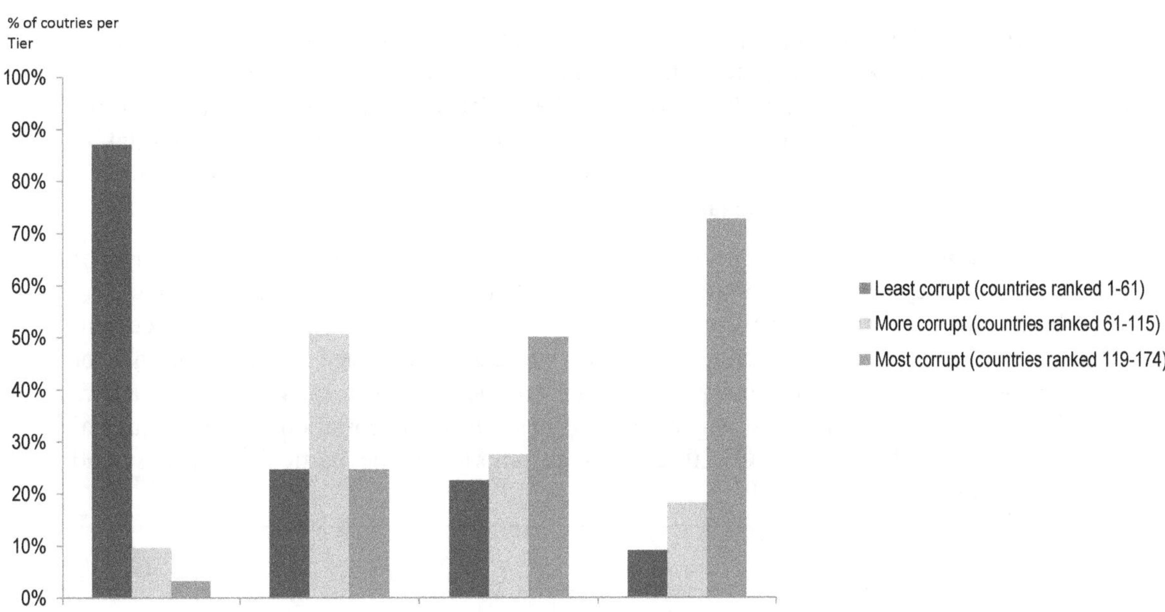

Note:

Tier 1: Countries whose governments fully comply with the Trafficking Victims Protection Act's (TVPA) minimum standards.

Tier 2: Countries whose governments do not fully comply with the TVPA's minimum standards, but are making significant efforts to bring themselves into compliance with those standards.

Tier 2 Watch List: Countries whose governments do not fully comply with the TVPA's minimum standards, but are making significant efforts to bring themselves into compliance with those standards and:

a) The absolute number of victims of severe forms of trafficking is very significant or is significantly increasing.
b) There is a failure to provide evidence of increasing efforts to combat severe forms of trafficking in persons from the previous year; or
c) The determination that a country is making significant efforts to bring itself into compliance with minimum standards was based on commitments by the country to take additional future steps over the next year.

Tier 3: Countries whose governments do not fully comply with the minimum standards and are not making significant efforts to do so.

Source: Author's own calculations, based on information from Transparency International (2014), *Corruption Perceptions Index 2014*, Transparency International, Berlin, http://files.transparency.org/content/download/1856/12434/file/2014_CPIBrochure_EN.pdf; US Department of State (2014), *Trafficking in Persons Report June 2014*, US Department of State, Washington, DC.

Moreover, there is a significant relationship between perceived levels of corruption and trafficking in persons. Traffickers may use high levels of perceived corruption to their advantage in the recruitment of victims, and to control them (UNODC, 2011). Victims who perceive corruption to be high are less likely to doubt a trafficker who claims middle men are required to obtain a visa, passport or other travel documents (UNODC, 2011). Similarly, a high level of perceived corruption in the victim's home country is also a powerful tool used by traffickers to control their victims in countries of destination. Traffickers often threaten victims that attempt to escape will be useless as corrupt police would bring them back to their exploiters. If victims have experienced corruption or have a perception of high levels of corruption in their home countries, they are more likely to believe these statements (UNODC, 2011).

When in the trafficking chain does corruption take place? Who are the corrupt actors? What are the corrupt acts?

Several studies have identified opportunities for corruption at various stages in the trafficking chain, who the potentially corrupt actors are, and what corrupt acts they commonly perform. Corrupt behaviour in the trafficking chain ranges from active involvement (such as violating duties, accepting or transferring bribes, and facilitating transactions), to passive involvement (such as ignoring or failing to follow up on information that a crime may be taking place).

The Council of Europe provides a general overview of professionals at risk of corruption. They range from public officials such as police, customs, consular and embassy officers, to border control, immigration services, other law enforcement agencies, local officials, intelligence/security forces and armed forces (national or international) to persons/groups/parties with "influence". The private sector actors include workers within travel agencies, airlines, the transportation sector, financial institutions, and banks (PACO, 2002). Risk is reported to be particularly widespread among police (Box 2.1).

Box 2.1. Cases of corruption identified by the Council of Europe among police

The Council of Europe has identified a number of recurring problems of corruption among police.

Police departments in charge of registering foreign citizens are believed to sometimes accept bribes to issue work and residence permits for foreign "dancers". Corrupt officials may issue identity documents as well as visas. This sometimes also involves corrupt staff of "western" embassies. Corruption at border crossings may also lead to the provision of entry visas and residence and work permits, or entry without control of travel documents. Corruption also involves the private sector, in particular travel agencies.

Police departments may collaborate with traffickers to put victims who have been arrested or are under protection back on the streets so that they can be re-trafficked or are prevented from giving testimony, or deport victims before they can give a testimony. There are reports of victims who return home that are re-trafficked immediately with the help of corrupt law enforcement officers or on the basis of information provided to traffickers by officers.

International police and armed forces may not only be customers, but there are cases where they are allegedly involved in trafficking and sexual exploitation. However, immunity prevents them from being prosecuted.

Local police as well as political authorities allegedly provide protection to business owners who use trafficked persons as forced labour in exchange for money or sexual services. There are instances where police officers earn supplementary income as security guards in clubs, bars and other establishments. This position enables them to inform business owners before raids and provide advance notice of planned police raids.

Source: PACO (2002), "Trafficking in human beings and corruption", Council of Europe, Report on the Regional Seminar, Portoroz, Slovenia, 19-22 June, p. 10 and p. 28.

Similarly to the Council of Europe, UNODC (2011) has identified a number of areas where corruption in the public sector furthers trafficking in persons:

- Traffickers may recruit, transport and exploit their victims with the help of corrupt public officials.
- Lack of investigation, prosecution and adjudication of trafficking in persons due to corrupt criminal justice officials.
- Lack of information and data collection on, as well as reporting of, trafficking-in-persons-related corruption.
- Protection of victims of trafficking impeded by corrupt public officials (and/or civil society actors).
- Lack of adequate responses to root causes of trafficking in persons.
- Lack of adequate response against major impediments to adequate criminal justice response.

In addition to these overarching challenges and problems, the Council of Europe and UNODC have identified and divided the key risks of corruption into three different stages of the trafficking cycle: the trafficking chain, the criminal justice chain and the victims support and protection stage (Table 2.1).

Transparency International (2011) has identified opportunities for corruption in the recruitment, transportation and exploitation phases of trafficking. According to Transparency International, corruption in the recruitment phase most likely takes the form of buying the silence of government bodies with responsibility for protecting society from recruitment for trafficking actions. In the transportation phase, corruption is most likely (and profitable) during border crossings. Border crossings provide the entry point for the involvement of additional actors, such as law enforcement bodies and other public officials. In the exploitation phase of trafficking, traffickers commonly rely on networks of trusted hotel owners or lessors of lodging. Often, these owners pay bribes or are offered bribes to allow trafficking to take place on the premises unchecked by law enforcement agencies. If raids or arrest happens, bribes may be paid to the police, prosecutors or judges in return for compromising the integrity of a successful investigation or prosecution of traffickers.

Table 2.1. **When, who and what identified by UNODC and the Council of Europe in the trafficking chains**

	Trafficking in persons chain	Criminal justice chain	Protection and support of victims
When	The trafficking chain consists of the recruitment of victims, the provision of documentation (identity papers, visas, permits), the transport of victims, which may include border-crossing, their exploitation, as well as the laundering of the proceeds of the crime.	The criminal justice chain ranges from the drafting and adoption of legislation, to crime prevention measures, preliminary investigations and investigations into specific offences, the search and seizure of proceeds, prosecution, trial and verdict, confiscation of proceeds, and enforcement of sanctions.	This protection and support of victims stage includes the provision of support, protection and shelter to victims of trafficking in persons.
Who	Corrupt actors within this chain of activities may include police, customs officers, visa officers or embassy staff, border control authorities, immigration services, other law enforcement agencies, intelligence/security services, armed forces (national or international), local officials, persons/groups/parties with influence on public officials, as well as private sector actors, such as travel agencies, airlines, transportation sector, financial institutions, and banks.	Corrupt actors may include parliamentarians, government officials, police, customs border control, immigration services and other law enforcement agencies, prosecutors, investigative judges, intelligence/security forces, local officials, as well as persons/groups, parties with influence on public officials.	Actors involved may include non-governmental organisations (NGOs) and civil society organisations, as well as public social service institutions.
What	Corrupt acts may range from passivity (ignoring or tolerating trafficking), or actively participating in or even organising trafficking in human beings, that is, from a violation of duties, to corruption or organised crime.	Acts pointing to corruption or organised crime, or at least to a violation of duties, may range from passivity (ignoring, tolerating, avoiding action) to an active obstruction of investigations, prosecution and judicial proceedings, the revealing and selling of information, and the perverting of the course of justice. Lack of awareness, capacities and skills may cause such behaviour, which may range from mere violation of duties to corruption and involvement in organised crime.	Corrupt behaviour may range from passivity and "trade-offs" (passivity in order not to compromise access to victims or co-operation with official institutions), to revealing or selling information on victims, betraying victims, or that an organisation is infiltrated by traffickers.

Source: UNODC (2011), *The Role of Corruption in Trafficking in Persons*, United Nations, Vienna, p. 7.

References

Holmes, L. (2009), "Human trafficking and corruption: Triple victimization?", in C. Friesendorf (ed.), *Strategies Against Human Trafficking: The Role of the Security Sector*, National Defence Academy and Austrian Ministry of Defence and Sports, Vienna, pp. 83-114.

IACC (International Anti-Corruption Conference) (2010), "WS#7 Corruption and Human Trafficking: Unraveling the Undistinguishable for a Better Fight", long workshop report, 14th International Anti-Corruption Conference 2010, Bangkok, Thailand, 10-13 November.

PACO (Programme Against Corruption and Organised Crime in South-Eastern Europe) (2002), "Trafficking in human beings and corruption", Council of Europe, Report on the Regional Seminar, Portoroz, Slovenia, 19-22 June.

Transparency International (2014), *Corruption Perceptions Index 2014*, Transparency International, Berlin, http://files.transparency.org/content/download/1856/12434/file/2014_CPIBrochure_EN.pdf.

Transparency International (2011), "Corruption and human trafficking", *Working Paper* 03/2011, Transparency International, Berlin.

Tremblay, M. (2010), "Corruption and Human Trafficking: Unraveling the Undistinguishable for a Better Fight", IACC 2010 workshop report, International Anti-Corruption Conference, Bangkok, Thailand, 10-13 November.

UNODC (United Nations Office on Drugs and Crime) (2011), *The Role of Corruption in Trafficking in Persons*, United Nations, Vienna.

UNODC (2008), *Toolkit to Combat Trafficking in Persons*, United Nations, New York, www.unodc.org/documents/human-trafficking/Toolkit-files/07-89375_Ebook[1].pdf.

US Department of State (2014), *Trafficking in Persons Report June 2014*, US Department of State, Washington, DC.

Chapter 3

The Guiding Principles on Combatting Corruption related to Trafficking in Persons

Despite the close link between trafficking in persons (TIP) and corruption, there have – up until this report – not been any international instruments that aim to address these two issues jointly. This chapter presents a set of "Guiding Principles on Combatting Corruption related to Trafficking in Persons" that can guide countries intending to establish, modify or complement a framework to address TIP-related corruption.

Organised trafficking requires systematic corruption. Addressing trafficking in persons (TIP) and corruption jointly is more effective in combatting TIP-related corruption than addressing the two topics separately. The APEC Pathfinder Dialogue on "Combating Corruption and Illicit Trade across the Asia-Pacific Region" that took place in Bangkok on 23-25 September 2013, the APEC Pathfinder Dialogue II on "Strengthening the Fight Against Corruption and Illicit Trade – Partnerships for Sustainable Security" that took place in Cebu City on 26 August 2015, and the "OECD Roundtable on Combatting Corruption related to Trafficking in Persons" that took place in Cebu City on 27 August 2015 confirmed the close link between trafficking in persons and corruption, and highlighted the importance of a sound integrity framework to combat this phenomenon.

A number of countries are party to a trafficking convention (see Table 1.4 in Chapter 1) or to an anti-corruption convention. However, despite the close link between trafficking in persons and corruption, there is – up until now – no international instrument that comprehensively focuses on the important link between corruption and trafficking in persons and that aims at addressing both. This approach of addressing these two issues jointly, coupled with better cross-border co-operation, better enforcement and an increased focus on combatting corruption is key to effectively curbing trafficking in persons.

In past studies a number of gaps in preventing and combating trafficking in persons and corruption and corresponding recommendations have been identified. This section highlights the main points raised and a set of corresponding principles that can facilitate the combating of TIP-related corruption. The following Guiding Principles can provide reference for countries intending to establish, modify or complement a framework to address TIP-related corruption.

1. International co-operation and agreements

Relevant international conventions are ratified and international co-operation against corruption and trafficking in persons is promoted.

In order to address the issue of trafficking in persons efficiently, there is a need to strengthen the legal basis against corruption and trafficking in persons. This could be done by strengthening international co-operation, and by countries joining international conventions and monitoring systems. It is important that national legislation on counter-trafficking is in line with international standards concerning trafficking in persons and corruption.

Processes of international co-operation in terms of mutual legal assistance and extradition are in place and functioning.

Trafficking in persons is often transnational in nature, with 66% of detected victims being trafficked across borders (UNODC, 2014). However, the criminal justice responses to trafficking in persons generally only operate within national borders. Therefore, to efficiently be able to respond to trafficking in persons, countries would benefit from effective processes of international co-operation in terms of mutual legal assistance and extradition. An example of an initiative aimed at achieving this is the "ASEAN Handbook on International Legal Cooperation in Trafficking in Persons Cases" (ASEAN,

2010) for the ASEAN region. In order to be efficient, mutual legal assistance must allow for international identification, sequestration and seizure of assets accrued by traffickers, and the procedure of mutual legal assistance should be simplified, prioritised, and accelerated. Examples of how to improve cross-border co-operation could be to link regional trafficking-in-persons focal points with regional anti-corruption focal points, and to identify and propose countermeasures to at-risk points of regional or transnational trafficking-in-persons-related corruption (for example the issuance of travel documents, border transfers and work permits). Law enforcement agencies should be encouraged to proactively share intelligence on transnational TIP networks. Law enforcement co-operation on intelligence is often an essential prerequisite to effective investigations, and it plays a complementary role to mutual legal assistance and subsequent prosecutions.

2. Jointly addressing and investigating trafficking in persons and corruption with particular focus on at-risk sectors

Strategies that address trafficking in persons and corruption, or include corruption issues in anti-trafficking plans, and vice versa, are in place.

Organised trafficking requires systemic corruption. However, few laws or strategies in place jointly address trafficking in persons and corruption. Due to the strong link between corruption/perceived levels of corruption with trafficking in persons (UNODC, 2011), countries are therefore recommended to put in place strategies that jointly address corruption and trafficking in persons, or alternatively include corruption issues in anti-trafficking plans, and vice versa. By streamlining approaches, countries can address the issue by modifying anti-corruption tools or by simply including corruption issues in existing anti-trafficking measures, in particular in trainings and strategies. The importance of ensuring sufficient levels of political will to combat trafficking-in-persons-related corruption at all levels of government should not be underestimated, and the implementation of the laws in place needs to be prioritised.

Sectors prone to trafficking-in-persons-related corruption are given priority in the implementation of relevant strategies.

When implementing the relevant strategies that address trafficking-in-persons-related corruption, countries are advised to identify and pay particular attention to vulnerable sectors and industries in their specific country context and steps that could be taken to prevent or combat the exploitation of people. This could, for example, entail regulation of labour-intensive sectors, in particular the construction, brothel, agriculture, fishing and textile industries or the foreign labour recruitment sector in a country. Countries are recommended to involve non-governmental actors as well as the private sector in the identification of at-risk sectors and the monitoring of these.

Information and resources are leveraged and shared among relevant actors.

Cases of trafficking and corruption are often dealt with separately. According to the United Nations Office on Drugs and Crime (UNODC), there is a lack of referral to the relevant authorities of 1) cases of trafficking in persons where there are indicators for corruption; and 2) referral of corruption cases where there are indicators of trafficking in persons. Co-operation is therefore essential among relevant actors to share information and resources. This can be done through the establishment of taskforces or joint operations. It is also crucial to establish protocols between non-governmental organisations (NGOs) and law enforcement bodies to co-ordinate their activities so that both sides understand and acknowledge the efforts and responsibilities of the other.

Furthermore, anti-money laundering systems can be used to detect and prevent the financing of trafficking in persons, and assist in the confiscation of profits from trafficking in persons as well as the prevention of the reinvestment of illicit funds into the criminal trafficking networks. Financial intelligence systems that are already in place can be used to map the activities of trafficking networks and how these networks interact with corrupt officials.

Corruption is also investigated when investigating trafficking in persons.

According to the Council of Europe, investigations and prosecutions of trafficking in persons should be accompanied by investigations into corruption and finances of suspects (PACO, 2002). In order to effectively deal with trafficking-in-persons-related corruption, indicators need to be developed for actors working in the field of trafficking in persons to detect corruption when investigating trafficking cases.

Specialised multi-agency units are established and multi-agency trainings are organised.

At the national level, countries could enhance co-operation between anti-corruption and anti-trafficking practitioners, for example through multi-agency training and specialised multi-agency units staffed by prosecutors and selected police.

3. Transparency and an integrity framework for public officials at risk

Specific rules/standards of behaviour – such as guidelines or codes of conduct – with respect to corruption and trafficking for public officials at risk are in place. The violations of the codes of conduct entail sanctions.

The conduct of the international peacekeepers, civilian police, intergovernmental and non-governmental organisations' staff and diplomatic personnel has raised serious concerns in relation to trafficking in persons and corruption (PACO, 2002). According to the cases analysed by the Council of Europe, the problem is reported to be particularly widespread among the police (PACO, 2002). One way of addressing this can be to include specific rules/standards of behaviour with respect to corruption and trafficking, for example, in codes of conduct. As supervision, discipline, and accountability are key in preventing and combating corruption, effective mechanisms are needed for reporting, investigating and sanctioning the violation of these codes of conduct for officials at risk.

Many of the sectors of public officials that could play a role in trafficking in persons are already covered by codes of conduct. However, some of these codes may need to be updated in order to address the specific issues relating to trafficking in persons. UNODC has proposed a number of specific measures that countries can implement, for example requesting police staff who are conducting brothel raids to always be accompanied by one or more colleagues, preferably female staff, when conducting raids in brothels (UNODC, 2011).

The activities of staff working in sectors at risk are performed in a transparent manner.

Sectors at specific risk of corruption in the trafficking-in-persons context need to ensure that their staff's activities are performed in a transparent manner and that unnecessary bureaucracy is eliminated so that the opportunities for corrupt officials to seek bribes are limited. This is particularly relevant within law enforcement (e.g. border control, customs and immigration authorities) and criminal justice authorities. As raised by UNODC, ensuring that the staff's activities are performed in a transparent manner does not necessarily mean public disclosure of assets and private interests but rather safeguards, such as, for example, internal approval systems of tasks to be performed and avoiding having one-to-one meetings with individuals such as visa and work permit applicants, presumed trafficking victims, and suspects (UNODC, 2011). In addition, independent legal audit of trafficking cases could be conducted in order to assure that cases were handled in a correct manner.

A wider framework of integrity for public officials is promoted.

In addition to establishing rules/standards on behaviour of public officials in respect to corruption and trafficking, countries can benefit from promoting a wider framework ensuring the integrity of public officials, including: asset disclosure regime; conflict-of-interest legislation; and whistleblower protection. Of particular focus are issues such as outside positions for police officers (for example, when police officers take up positions as security guards for bars and clubs). Officials at risk should also receive general anti-corruption training that could contribute to the prevention and combating of corruption in trafficking in persons. These need to be context specific and address potential issues such as cultures of corruption and gift-giving.

Mechanisms that allow for public officials as well as the public to expose misconduct and report dishonest or illegal activity and that ensure the effective protection from retaliation are in place.

Confidential hotlines or similar measures for whistleblowers may be established so that public officials or private sector employees that witness corrupt behaviour by their colleagues can provide information about these activities. This can be established within government organisations as well as international organisations. Members of the public may also be given clear channels for exposing misconduct and reporting dishonest or illegal activity occurring in public and private sector organisations. Countries need to ensure that whistleblowers are effectively protected from retaliation and intimidation.

The recruitment process of officials is transparent, competitive and subject to independent scrutiny. Upon recruitment, officials receive training, adequate supervision and are subject to regular performance evaluations.

Recruitment of key officials, in particular those employed in anti-corruption or anti-trafficking units, prosecutors and judicial officials needs to consistently be conducted by the means of a transparent and competitive selection process that is subject to independent scrutiny. Upon recruitment, key officials would benefit from receiving training, adequate supervision and be subject to regular performance evaluations. It is important that the training does not only cover instructions relating to specific tasks and responsibilities that the employee will encounter, but also the standards of conduct and values of the organisation.

Key officials receive training so that they are able to correctly identify trafficking victims, understand the nature of the crime, and recognise warning signs throughout the different stages of the trafficking-in-persons process.

In order to correctly identify and deal with trafficking-in-persons cases, it is essential that key officials receive training. Experience shows that the first government official a victim of trafficking is likely to meet is a local police officer and not a lawmaker or diplomat, and if this local police officer has not been trained to identify trafficking victims and understand the crime, there is a heightened risk that the crime is not properly identified (US Department of State, 2012). Also, for example consular staff in countries of origin may benefit from exchanging experiences and being trained in recognising visa applications that could involve trafficking in persons.

4. Awareness-raising and prevention measures for public officials and the general public

Public awareness regarding the existence, causes, and gravity of trafficking in persons and the active participation of individuals and groups outside the public sector in the prevention of, and the fight against, trafficking-in-persons-related corruption is promoted.

The importance of prevention measures is not consistently recognised. Article 13 of the United Nations Convention against Corruption (UNCAC) (United Nations, 2003) demands that each State Party shall take the appropriate measures to promote the "active participation of individuals and groups outside the public sector, such as civil society, non-governmental organisations and community-based organisations, in the prevention of and the fight against corruption and to raise public awareness regarding the existence, causes and gravity of and the threat posed by corruption." Specific measures to strengthen this participation include:

1. enhancing the transparency of, and promoting the contribution of, the public to decision-making processes
2. ensuring that the public has effective access to information
3. undertaking public information activities that contribute to non-tolerance of corruption, as well as public education programmes, including school and university curricula
4. respecting, promoting and protecting the freedom to seek, receive, publish and disseminate information concerning corruption.

Similarly, Article 9(2) of the United Nations (2000) "Protocol to Prevent, Suppress and Punish Trafficking in Persons, Especially Women and Children" establishes that State Parties shall "endeavour to undertake such measures such as research, information and mass media campaigns and social and economic initiatives to prevent and combat trafficking in persons." The Council of Europe suggests giving particular attention to the development of special awareness programmes in schools (PACO, 2002).

In order to effectively raise awareness of the linkages between corruption and trafficking in persons, countries can involve and train media and facilitate investigative journalism on trafficking in persons and corruption. Furthermore, media can play an important role in increasing public awareness and knowledge on TIP and corruption hotspots, deterring offenders by highlighting arrests and prosecutions, and rewarding and encouraging successful law enforcement through the publication of success stories.

Targeted awareness-raising measures for all parties involved in anti-trafficking issues are provided.

In addition to general anti-corruption measures, specific awareness-raising measures that highlight vulnerabilities, responsibilities, risks, and draw attention to how corrupt behaviour could facilitate the crime of trafficking in persons and the re-victimisation of the trafficked victims are essential to understand the links and forms of trafficking. Consequently, these measures need to be provided for all parties involved in anti-trafficking issues, including police and anti-trafficking organisations.

Preventive measures for potential victims of trafficking in persons are in place, in particular offering counselling about corruption and trafficking before and after they have undertaken a migration journey and alerting communities of early signs of corruption.

It is essential to build civic response and community awareness about the linkages between corruption and trafficking in persons. Specific measures proposed by the UNODC for potential victims of trafficking includes: 1) alerting communities that early signs of corruption in a legitimate migration journey should be considered as warning indicators that trafficking may be taking place; and 2) giving citizens access to free, confidential counselling about corruption and trafficking before and after they have undertaken a migration journey, in order to make them aware of their rights and capable of looking for help if they are infringed in a way that renders them victims of trafficking (UNODC, 2011).

5. Improvement of data collection and systematic use of information

Data on trafficking in persons are collected, analysed and used systematically.

Most countries are not systematically collecting and analysing data on investigations or prosecutions of public officials relating to trafficking in persons and corruption (UNODC, 2011). There are many reasons for the scarcity of data. Among the most important reasons highlighted by the International Organization for Migration (IOM) are the victims' reluctance to report or testify for fear of reprisals; lack of harmonisation among existing data sources; and the opposition of some countries and agencies to share data (Laczko, 2002). As a crucial step in addressing trafficking-in-persons-related corruption, countries need to focus on the collection of data and information in order to get a better insight into the problem. Because of its transnational nature, data on trafficking-in-persons-related corruption also needs to be collected and aggregated at the regional level. It should be stressed that any legal provisions or policy decisions on data collection and/or the creation of databases need to be accompanied by a commitment of resources for implementation.

Information on corruption provided by victims and NGOs can also be used more systematically. Government agencies working on anti-corruption and anti-trafficking need to co-operate with the non-governmental sector and civil society to ensure that information and experiences from victims are collected (through, for example, interviews) and that this information is passed on to the anti-corruption and anti-trafficking units in government. By improving the data collection and systemic use of information, countries would be allowed to implement targeted responses based on facts.

6. Lift immunity in corruption and trafficking cases

Immunity from prosecution of public officials is duly lifted to allow for effective investigation, prosecution and adjudication of corruption and trafficking-in-persons-related offences.

The purpose of immunity is to protect the independence of public officials and make sure that they will make difficult decisions without risking facing personal consequences for this decision (e.g. being sued). According to UNCAC Article 30(2), "Each State Party shall take such measures as may be necessary to establish or maintain, in accordance with its legal system and constitutional principles, an appropriate balance between any immunities or jurisdictional privileges accorded to its public officials for the performance of their functions and the possibility, when necessary, of effectively investigating, prosecuting and adjudicating offences established in accordance with this Convention." Similarly, in cases of trafficking in persons, countries need to lift the immunity from prosecution of public officials following an allegation of corruption that is supported by evidence.

References

ASEAN (Association of Southeast Asian Nations) (2010), *ASEAN Handbook on International Legal Cooperation in Trafficking in Persons Cases*, ASEAN Secretariat, Jakarta, www.unodc.org/documents/human-trafficking/ASEAN_Handbook_on_International_Legal_Cooperation_in_TIP_Cases.pdf.

Laczko, F. (2002), "Human Trafficking: The Need for Better Data", *Migration Information Source*, Migration Policy Institute, www.migrationinformation.org/feature/display.cfm?ID=66.

PACO (Programme Against Corruption and Organised Crime in South-Eastern Europe) (2002), "Trafficking in human beings and corruption", Council of Europe, Report on the Regional Seminar, Portoroz, Slovenia, 19-22 June.

United Nations (2003), "United Nations Convention against Corruption", *United Nations Treaty Series*, Vol. 2349, No. 42146, New York, 31 October, p. 41, https://treaties.un.org/doc/Publication/UNTS/Volume%202349/v2349.pdf.

United Nations (2000), "Protocol to Prevent, Suppress and Punish Trafficking in Persons, Especially Women and Children, supplementing the United Nations Convention against Transnational Organized Crime", *Treaty Collection*, database, https://treaties.un.org/Pages/ViewDetails.aspx?src=IND&mtdsg_no=XVIII-12-a&chapter=18&lang=en.

UNODC (United Nations Office on Drugs and Crime) (2014), *Global Report on Trafficking in Persons 2014*, United Nations, New York, www.unodc.org/documents/data-and-analysis/glotip/GLOTIP_2014_full_report.pdf.

UNODC (2011), *The Role of Corruption in Trafficking in Persons*, United Nations, Vienna.

US Department of State (2012), *Trafficking in Persons Report June 2012*, US Department of State, Washington, DC.

Chapter 4

Testing the Guiding Principles on Combatting Corruption related to Trafficking in Persons in the Philippines

This chapter takes stock of the potential practical application of the "Guiding Principles on Combatting Corruption related to Trafficking in Persons" in the context of the Philippines, and explores whether the Guiding Principles effectively address the concerns identified in relation to trafficking in persons and corruption.

With the goal of ensuring that the "Guiding Principles on Combatting Corruption related to Trafficking in Persons" (hereafter, the Guiding Principles) are both relevant and useful in addressing the real-life, practical challenges identified on the ground in relation to trafficking in persons (TIP) and corruption, the Guiding Principles were tested in the Philippines. The first part of the chapter will introduce the legal and institutional framework in place and the general situation in relation to TIP and corruption in the Philippines. The second part of the chapter will highlight how the issues raised in the respective principles have been applied in the context of the Philippines – and/or, if relevant, discuss any challenges or lessons learned in addressing the issues raised in the principles in question. The final part of the chapter will present the feedback on the Guiding Principles provided by stakeholders that were consulted during an OECD fact-finding mission to Manila in August 2015, and the findings from the in-country testing.

The legal framework

The Philippines "Anti-Trafficking in Persons Act of 2003 (R.A. 9208)" (Republic of the Philippines, 2003a) and the "Expanded Anti-Trafficking in Persons Act of 2012 (R.A. 10364)" (Republic of the Philippines, 2012a) that amends R.A. No. 9208 are the primary laws in place on trafficking in persons. Section 4 defines acts of trafficking in persons as recruiting, transporting, transferring, harbouring, receiving, maintaining, obtaining, hiring, providing or offering a person, by non-violent or violent means, for the purpose of sexual (prostitution, acts of lasciviousness, pornography, sex tourism), labour (forced labour, slavery, debt bondage, involuntary servitude), or organ exploitation (removal or sale of organs).

In the "Expanded Anti-Trafficking in Persons Act of 2012 (R.A. 10364)", the Philippines included the issues of trafficking-in-persons-related corruption in a number of sections. For example, Section 8 amending Section 5(h) makes it illegal "to tamper or cause the destruction of evidence or influence or attempt to influence witnesses in an investigation or prosecution", and the amendments to Paragraph 5(j) make it illegal "to utilise his or her office to impede investigation, prosecution or execution of lawful order." Violations of these paragraphs will lead to a penalty of 15 years in prison and a fine between PHP 500 000 and PHP 1 million. Section 9 amending Section 6 defines qualified trafficking as when the offender is a member of the military or law enforcement agencies. The penalty for qualified trafficking is life in prison and a fine between PHP 2 million and PHP 5 million. Section 12 amending Section 10(j) stipulates that "Any employee or official of government agencies who shall issue or approve the issuance of travel exit clearances, passports, registration certificates, counselling certificates, marriage license, and other similar documents to persons, whether juridical or natural, recruitment agencies, establishments or other individuals or groups, who fail to observe the prescribed procedures and the requirement as provided for by laws, rules and regulations, shall be held administratively liable, without prejudice to criminal liability under this Act. The concerned government official or employee shall, upon conviction, be dismissed from the service and be barred permanently to hold public office. His or her retirement and other benefits shall likewise be forfeited." Finally, Section 13 that amends Section 11 addresses the demand side of trafficking. If the offender is a public official, the Act stipulates that "he or she shall be dismissed from service and shall suffer perpetual absolute disqualification to hold public, office, in addition to any imprisonment or fine received pursuant to any other provision of this Act."

In addition to the "Anti-Trafficking in Persons Act of 2003 (R.A. 9208)" and the "Expanded Anti-Trafficking in Persons Act of 2012", there are also a number of related laws that address trafficking in persons, including:

- "R.A. 10365 – "An Act Further Strengthening The Anti-Money Laundering Law, Amending For The Purpose 'Republic Act No. 9160', Otherwise Known As The 'Anti-Money Laundering Act Of 2001', As Amended" (Republic of the Philippines, 2012b) – where the amendments includes trafficking in persons as a crime that is covered by the Act, thereby making it possible to go after the money of traffickers.
- The "Migrant Workers and Overseas Filipinos Act of 1995, as amended by R.A. 10022 in 2009" (Republic of the Philippines, 2009a) – which strengthens the protection provided to overseas Filipino workers, and provides for their repatriation, prohibits reprocessing or changes to their contracts, establishes a policy against illegal recruitment and regulates the ownership of recruitment agencies.
- "R.A. 6955 – An Act to Declare Unlawful the Practice of Matching Filipino Women for Marriage to Foreign Nationals on a Mail Order Basis and Other Similar Practices, Including the Advertisement, Publication, Printing or Distribution of Brochures, Fliers and Other Propaganda Materials in Furtherance Thereof and Providing Penalty Therefore" (Republic of the Philippines, 1990).
- "R.A. 8043 – An Act Establishing the Rules to Govern Inter-Country Adoption of Filipino Children, and for Other Purposes" (Republic of the Philippines, 1995a).
- The "Special Protection of Children against Child Abuse, Exploitation and Discrimination Act (R.A. 7610) of 1992 as amended by R.A. 9231" (Republic of the Philippines, 2003b) – which restricts employment of children that are under 15 years old and prohibits the worst forms of child labour, such as slavery, sale and trafficking or children, procuring, offering or exposing of a child for prostitution, for the production of pornography or for pornographic performances.
- "R.A. 9995 – An Act Defining and Penalising the Crime of Photo and Video Voyeurism, Prescribing Penalties Therefor, and for Other Purposes" (Republic of the Philippines, 2009b).
- The "Anti-Child Pornography Act of 2009 (R.A. 9775)" (Republic of the Philippines, 2009c) - that seeks to protect children "from all forms of exploitation and abuse including, but not limited to: 1) the use of a child in pornographic performances and materials; and 2) the inducement or coercion of a child to engage or be involved in pornography through whatever means."
- The "Revised Penal Code, as Amended" (Republic of the Philippines, 1930) - where Title 7, Chapter 2, Section 2 deals with crimes committed by public officers, focusing in particular on bribery in relation to agreeing to perform certain acts or refraining from prosecuting or arresting offenders in consideration of any offer, promise, gift or present.

In relation to corruption, the legislative responses to criminal acts where the offender is a public official are regulated through a number of laws. The "Anti-Graft and Corrupt Practices Act (R.A. 3019)" defines what constitutes corrupt acts and the penalties for violations; the requirements of assets and liabilities disclosure; and the penalties for unexplained wealth. The "Anti-Graft and Corrupt Practices Act" can be used together with the anti-trafficking acts (R.A. 9208 and R.A. 10364). The Act establishing a "Code of Conduct and Ethical Standards for Public Officials and Employees (R.A. 6713)" (Republic of the Philippines, 1989a) defines the norms of conduct of public officials and employees, the duties of public officials and employees, prohibited acts and transactions (focusing, for example, on conflicts of interests and outside employment), and requirements to disclose and submit statements on assets and liabilities. Other examples include the "Act Defining and Penalizing the Crime of Plunder (R.A. 7080)" (Republic of the Philippines, 1991a) where public officers have acquired ill-gotten wealth of at least PHP 50 million, "An Act Declaring Forfeiture In Favor Of The State Any Property Found To Have Been Unlawfully Acquired By Any Public Officer Or Employee And Providing For The Proceedings Therefor (R.A. 1379)" (Republic of the Philippines, 1955), and "Presidential Decree 46" (Republic of the Philippines, 1972), making it punishable for public officials and employees to receive – and for private persons to give – gifts on any occasion.

During the interviews conducted by the OECD in Manila in August 2015, representatives from government agencies and civil society organisations alike highlighted that the legal framework in place is very good – some even said close to perfect – but that there are serious problems in relation to its implementation. This was reported to be particularly problematic at the local level. For example, there were reports of public officials not having knowledge of the legal framework in place, or if they were aware, they chose to ignore it. One government representative also stated that the law builds upon an ideal that is sometimes hard to execute in the real world. Scholars have also argued that it is "the pervasive government corruption that prevents the proper implementation of programs, enforcement of laws, and prosecution of traffickers" (Guth, 2010, pp. 156-157).

The institutional framework

The Philippine "Anti-Trafficking in Persons Act" establishes an Inter-Agency Council Against Trafficking (IACAT). IACAT is co-chaired by the Secretary of the Department of Justice and the Secretary of the Department of Social Welfare and Development. In addition, IACAT is composed of representatives from the Department of Foreign Affairs, the Department of Labor and Employment, the Philippine Overseas Employment Administration, the Philippine National Police, the Bureau of Immigration, the Philippine Commission on Women, the National Bureau of Investigation, the Department of the Interior and Local Government, the Philippine Center on Transnational Crimes, the Council for the Welfare of Children, the Commission on Filipinos Overseas, and three representatives from non-governmental organisations (NGOs), where one NGO represents women, one NGO represents Filipinos, and one NGO represents children. The NGO representatives are appointed for a term of three years.

Through the creation of IACAT, the Philippines has adopted a multi-disciplinary and multi-stakeholder approach to combating trafficking in persons. IACAT is tasked with performing numerous functions, including: 1) formulating a comprehensive and integrated programme to prevent and suppress trafficking; 2) promulgating rules and regulations for the effective implementation of the "Anti-Trafficking in Persons Act"; 3) monitoring and overseeing the implementation of the Act; 4) co-ordinating the work of the various member agencies; and 5) co-ordinating awareness-raising and outreach activities. In regards to Point 1, the current "National Strategic Action Plan Against

Trafficking in Persons" – the second of its kind – covers the period 2012-16. IACAT is also required to develop a mechanism to ensure the timely, co-ordinated, and effective response to cases of trafficking in persons, to assist in the filing of cases, and to formulate a programme for victim reintegration together with concerned agencies.

According to IACAT, one of its best practices is the creation of a number of taskforces for combatting trafficking in persons. There are 23 taskforces across the Philippines that are composed of prosecutors who do case build-up. In addition, there are 15 regional anti-trafficking taskforces, 6 port-based inter-agency anti-trafficking taskforces, and 2 special national taskforces composed of prosecutors that operate nationally to be able to strike anywhere.

IACAT also has four support units: the temporary victims' shelter unit; the warrant taskforce; the cyber-trafficking unit; and the Operations Center. The Operations Center addresses the problem of locating witnesses or victims who do not want to come forward or testify, by, for example, establishing temporary shelter for witnesses and trafficking victims (US Department of State, 2013). The Operations Centre operates nationally and includes a quick reaction team that is composed of prosecutors, law enforcement officers, social welfare investigators and representatives from civil society organisations that can respond to calls from the IACAT hotline and conduct surveillance in suspected trafficking hotspots (United Nations, 2013; Inter-Agency Council Against Trafficking, 2012).

Although civil society stakeholders as well as government representatives report that IACAT and its taskforces are functioning well, there has been criticism regarding what the United Nations (UN) Special Rapporteur on Trafficking in Persons dubbed "a plethora of structures", making it "difficult to assess how they function in practice and to what extent each of them is useful and effective" (United Nations, 2013, p. 11). Moving forward, it would be useful if regular monitoring or a comprehensive evaluation of the functioning of the institutional set-up dealing with trafficking in persons in the Philippines were to be conducted.

The situation in the Philippines

According to the US Department of State's 2015 *Trafficking in Persons Report*, the Philippines "is a source country and, to a much lesser extent, a destination and transit country for men, women, and children subjected to sex trafficking and forced labor" (US Department of State, 2015, p. 279). Many of the 10 million Filipinos that live abroad and the estimated 1 million that migrate every year are subjected to forced labour and trafficking for sexual exploitation throughout Asia, Europe, the Middle East and North America (ILO, n.d.; US Department of State, 2015). According to the UN Special Rapporteur on Trafficking in Persons, trafficking for domestic servitude is one of the most prevalent forms of cross-border trafficking of Filipinos (United Nations, 2013). Filipinos that want to work abroad have to go through recruitment agencies, and these have to be licensed by the government. However, there have been reports of licensed recruitment agencies that have conducted illegal trafficking activities (Guth, 2010). Within the Philippines, major problems remain in relation to sex trafficking in the major cities and tourist destinations, as well as domestic servitude, forced begging and forced labour in factories (US Department of State, 2015). Men are mostly victims of forced labour and debt bondage in the agricultural, fishing, and maritime sectors (US Department of State, 2015).

In relation to corruption, the US Department of State reported in 2015 that "[p]ervasive corruption undermined government efforts to combat trafficking, and investigations of potentially complicit officials did not lead to criminal convictions and in some cases even failed to secure administrative punishment against offenders" (US Department of State, 2015, p. 280). Furthermore, it was stated that "[p]ublic officials, including those in diplomatic missions abroad, law enforcement agencies, and other government entities, are reported to be complicit in trafficking or allow traffickers to operate with impunity" (US Department of State, 2015, p. 280). The US Department of State (2015) also reported that "some corrupt officials accept payments or sexual services from establishments notorious for trafficking, accept bribes to facilitate illegal departures for overseas workers, downgrade trafficking charges, or overlook unscrupulous labor recruiters" and "conduct indiscriminate or fake raids on commercial sex establishments to extort money from managers, clients, and victims" (p. 280). In addition, the US Department of State (2015) stated that "[s]ome personnel working at Philippine embassies abroad reportedly sexually harass victims of domestic servitude, withhold back wages procured for them, subject them to domestic servitude for a second time, or coerce sexual acts in exchange for government protection services" (p. 280). Similar reports were given from civil society in the interviews conducted by the OECD in Manila in August 2015. Stakeholders highlighted that bribery remained a prominent issue and that pay-offs have resulted in limited apprehensions, prosecutions, and convictions. There were numerous anecdotal accounts from civil society on cases where witnesses had received pay-offs so that they would not testify in court, and other cases where police have been bribed not to file a case or pursue further investigations. In short, it has been argued that if human trafficking in the Philippines is to be significantly reduced, corruption must be curbed (Guth, 2010).

In relation to corruption, stakeholders interviewed highlighted that the culture of corruption is a systemic problem in the Philippines. There is also a deep-rooted culture of gift-giving. Although this has been regulated through the "Anti-Graft and Corrupt Practices Act", as well as the "Presidential Decree 46", which makes it punishable for public officials and employees to receive – and for private persons to give – gifts on any occasion, the problem remains. In the end, going after corruption also means going after a highly lucrative additional income that officials have gotten accustomed to. Reforming the civil service is a big task, and although there are reports of agencies trying to reform by offering incentives such as early retirement to get young blood into the organisation, these initiatives were unsuccessful when the young – or in other words not the intended target group for the incentives – accepted early retirement and went into the private sector instead. Moving forward, the government will need to continue devoting attention to its anti-corruption efforts. In regard to how these efforts could be improved, it was suggested that joint taskforces – similar to those that have been implemented for agencies working on trafficking in persons – could be established, thereby making it possible to hand-pick people of integrity and competence within their respective fields to ensure that the laws on anti-corruption are enforced.

In 2013, the UN Special Rapporteur on Trafficking in Persons reported that she did not receive "information on any criminal sanction having been instituted against officials facilitating the activities of traffickers" (United Nations, 2013, p. 19). Echoing this finding, the US Department of State's 2015 *Trafficking in Persons Report* included a recommendation for the Philippines to "[i]ncrease efforts to hold government officials administratively and criminally accountable for trafficking and trafficking-related offenses through criminal prosecutions, convictions, and stringent sentences" (p. 280).

There are some signs that situation is beginning to change, with a recent example from 2015 of a conviction against a Bureau of Immigration officer for allowing a passenger to pass through immigration inspection with fraudulent travel documents (Bureau of Immigration, 2015).

The Guiding Principles and the Philippines

This next part of the chapter will highlight how the issues raised in the respective principles have been applied in the context of the Philippines – and/or, if relevant, discuss any challenges or lessons learned in addressing the issues raised in the respective principles. Each sub-section will commence with a box stating the principle in question, followed by the application of it in the Philippines.

1. International co-operation and agreements

Relevant international conventions are ratified and international co-operation against corruption and trafficking in persons is promoted.

In order to address the issue of trafficking in persons efficiently, there is a need to strengthen the legal basis against corruption and trafficking in persons. This could be done by strengthening international co-operation, and by countries joining international conventions and monitoring systems. It is important that national legislation on counter-trafficking is in line with international standards concerning trafficking in persons and corruption.

The Philippines has ratified the United Nations "Protocol to Prevent, Suppress and Punish Trafficking in Persons, Especially Women and Children, supplementing the United Nations Convention against Transnational Organized Crime" (also known as the "Palermo Protocol") (United Nations, 2000) and the United Nations "Convention Against Corruption" (United Nations, 2003). The Philippines has also ratified several International Labour Organization (ILO) conventions, including the "Convention concerning Forced or Compulsory Labour (No. 29)" (ILO, 1930), the "Convention concerning the Abolition of Forced Labour (No. 105)" (ILO, 1957), the "Convention concerning the Prohibition and Immediate Action for the Elimination of the Worst Forms of Child Labour (No. 182)" (ILO, 1999), and the "Convention concerning Decent Work for Domestic Workers (No. 189)" (ILO, 2011).

In addition to UN and ILO conventions, the Philippines is also a signatory to the "ASEAN Declaration Against Trafficking in Persons Particularly Women and Children" (ASEAN, 2004a).

The "Manila Declaration to Enhance International Cooperation in Combating Human Trafficking" was signed at the First International Dialogue on Human Trafficking – a gathering that attracted 100 conference delegates from 19 embassies in the Philippines, 11 non-governmental organisations, and 15 government agencies (IACAT, 2015a). The Manila Declaration "recognized that there is an urgent need for a comprehensive international approach to prevent and combat human trafficking" and that "an effective international approach against human trafficking requires innovative actions in the face of changing schemes of perpetrators, along with continued dialogue, exchange of information through sanctioned channels and cooperation among stakeholders" (Canlas, 2015; IACAT, 2015a).

During the interviews conducted by the OECD in Manila in August 2015, government representatives highlighted that the various conventions that the Philippines has ratified have been useful in their fight against corruption. In particular, the "Palermo Protocol" was mentioned as the basis for the national "Anti-Trafficking in Persons Act".

Processes of international co-operation in terms of mutual legal assistance and extradition are in place and functioning.

Trafficking in persons is often transnational in nature, with 66% of detected victims being trafficked across borders. However, the criminal justice responses to trafficking in persons generally only operate within national borders. Therefore, to efficiently be able to respond to trafficking in persons, countries would benefit from effective processes of international co-operation in terms of mutual legal assistance and extradition. An example of an initiative aimed at achieving this is the "Handbook on International Cooperation in Trafficking in Persons Cases" (ASEAN, 2010) for the ASEAN region. In order to be efficient, mutual legal assistance must allow for international identification, sequestration and seizure of assets accrued by traffickers, and the procedure of mutual legal assistance should be simplified, prioritised, and accelerated. Examples of how to improve cross-border co-operation could be to link regional trafficking-in-persons-focal points with regional anti-corruption focal points, and to identify and propose countermeasures to at-risk points of regional or transnational trafficking-in-persons-related corruption (for example the issuance of travel documents, border transfers and work permits). Law enforcement agencies should be encouraged to proactively share intelligence on transnational TIP networks. Law enforcement co-operation on intelligence is often an essential prerequisite to effective investigations, and it plays a complementary role to mutual legal assistance and subsequent prosecutions.

The "Expanded Anti-Trafficking in Persons Act (R.A. 10364)" allows for extraterritorial jurisdiction and extradition. In relation to extradition, Section 23 states that "[t]he government may surrender or extradite persons accused of trafficking in the Philippines to the appropriate international court if any, or to another State pursuant to the applicable extradition laws and treaties."

In November 2004, the Philippines together with Brunei, Cambodia, Indonesia, Laos, Malaysia, Singapore and Viet Nam signed the "2004 Treaty on Mutual Legal Assistance in Criminal Matters among like-minded ASEAN Member Countries" (ASEAN, 2004b). Thailand and Myanmar signed it in 2006. The purpose of the treaty is to "improve the effectiveness of the law enforcement authorities of the Parties in the prevention, investigation and prosecution of offences through co-operation and mutual legal assistance in criminal matters." The Treaty states that Parties should "render to one another the widest possible measure of mutual legal assistance in criminal matters", specifying that requests should be channelled through a designated Central Authority in each country "to facilitate the orderly, effective and timely execution of requests for mutual legal assistance in criminal matters", and that the mutual legal assistance should be providing in a form that is useable and admissible in the requesting country.

In 2015, the US Department of State reported that "Philippine officials continued to co-operate with foreign governments to pursue international law enforcement action against suspected traffickers" (2015, p. 281), with six trafficking investigations of this kind being initiated in 2014. This was echoed in the interviews conducted in the Philippines in August 2015. Interviewed government representatives stated that co-operation has been improved, and that they were in regular contact with their foreign counterparts.

2. *Jointly addressing and investigating trafficking in persons and corruption with particular focus on at-risk sectors*

Strategies that address trafficking in persons and corruption, or include corruption issues in anti-trafficking plans, and vice versa, are in place.

Organised trafficking requires systemic corruption. However, few laws or strategies in place jointly address trafficking in persons and corruption. Due to the strong link between corruption/perceived levels of corruption with trafficking in persons, countries are therefore recommended to put in place strategies that jointly address corruption and trafficking in persons, or alternatively include corruption issues in anti-trafficking plans, and vice versa. By streamlining approaches, countries can address the issue by modifying anti-corruption tools or by simply including corruption issues in existing anti-trafficking measures, in particular in trainings and strategies. The importance of ensuring sufficient levels of political will to combat trafficking-in-persons-related corruption at all levels of government should not be underestimated, and the implementation of the laws in place needs to be prioritised.

As mentioned in a previous section on the legal framework in the Philippines, there are a number of provisions in the "Expanded Anti-Trafficking in Persons Act (RA. 10364)" that addresses corruption related to trafficking in persons. Section 8 amending Section 5 (h) makes it illegal "to tamper or cause the destruction of evidence or influence or attempt to influence witnesses in an investigation or prosecution" and Paragraph (j) makes it illegal "to utilize his or her office to impede investigation, prosecution or execution of lawful order." Violations of these paragraphs will lead to a penalty of 15 years in prison and a fine of between PHP 500 000 and PHP 1 million pesos. Section 9 amending Section 6 defines qualified trafficking as when the offender is a member of the military or law enforcement agencies. The penalty for qualified trafficking is life in prison and a fine between PHP 2 million and PHP 5 million. Section 12 amending Section 10(j) stipulates that "Any employee or official of government agencies who shall issue or approve the issuance of travel exit clearances, passports, registration certificates, counselling certificates, marriage licenses, and other similar documents to persons, whether juridical or natural, recruitment agencies, establishments or other individuals or groups, who fail to observe the prescribed procedures and the requirement as provided for by laws, rules and regulations, shall be held administratively liable, without prejudice to criminal liability under this Act. The concerned government official or employee shall, upon conviction, be dismissed from the service and be barred permanently to hold public office. His or her retirement and other benefits shall likewise be forfeited." Finally, Section 13 that amends Section 11 addresses the demand side of trafficking. If the offender is a public official, the Act stipulates that "he or she shall be dismissed from service and shall suffer perpetual absolute disqualification to hold public office, in addition to any imprisonment or fine received pursuant to any other provision of this Act."

In addition to the law, there are trainings conducted on ethical investigation and prosecution by IACAT/the Department of Justice, where parts of the module revisit the values that should be adhered to. Also, there have been trainings organised by NGOs that have focused on the issue of trafficking-in-persons-related corruption. Examples include a training for the Integrated Bar of the Philippines that was organised by the Visayan Forum Foundation, and a three-day training course organised by the Visayan Forum Foundation and the Inter-Agency Council Against Trafficking for frontline officers from the Ninoy Aquino International Airport and Diosdado Macapagal International Airport, the Bureau of Customs, the Bureau of Immigration, the National Bureau of Investigation, and the Philippine Overseas Employment Agency. These types of initiative could be scaled up in order to reach wider groups of public officials at risk.

Sectors prone to trafficking-in-persons-related corruption are given priority in the implementation of relevant strategies.

When implementing the relevant strategies that address trafficking-in-persons-related corruption, countries are advised to identify and pay particular attention to vulnerable sectors and industries in their specific country context and steps that could be taken to prevent or combat the exploitation of people. This could, for example, entail regulation of labour-intensive sectors, in particular the construction, brothel, agriculture, fishing and textile industries or the foreign labour recruitment sector in a country. Countries are recommended to involve non-governmental actors as well as the private sector in the identification of at-risk sectors and the monitoring of these.

The foreign labour recruitment sector is one of the at-risk sectors for trafficking-in-persons-related corruption in the Philippines. As previously highlighted, many of the 10 million Filipinos that live abroad, and the estimated 1 million that migrate every year, are subjected to forced labour and trafficking for sexual exploitation throughout Asia, Europe, the Middle East and North America (ILO, n.d.; US Department of State, 2015). Filipinos that want to work abroad have to go through recruitment agencies, and these have to be licensed by the Philippine Overseas Employment Agency (POEA). Although the recruitment agencies are licensed by the government in order to ensure that they are following the applicable rules and laws in place and that they are running legitimate businesses, there have been reports of corruption in relation to the issuance of these licenses to illegitimate employment agencies, as well as evidence of government officials changing the status of a suspended employment agency's license after the agency was found guilty of violating recruitment regulations (Guth, 2010). Regardless of the reports of corruption in changing the status of suspended employment agencies, several stakeholders highlighted POEA's blacklisting of employment agencies that are under investigation as a best practice that could be replicated in other countries facing similar problems.

Within the Philippines, at-risk sectors include sex trafficking, domestic servitude, forced begging and forced labour in factories for women and children, and forced labour and debt bondage in agricultural, fishing, and maritime sectors for men (United Nations, 2013). In the interviews conducted by the OECD in August 2015, civil society called for an increased focus from the government on forced labour in relation to agriculture, fisheries, and domestic servitude. Representatives from non-governmental sectors in the country stated that the government has so far mostly focused on sex trafficking, and that this will need to change. The data available supports this statement, with 93% of the convictions that have so far been secured under the "Anti-Trafficking in Persons Act" being sex-trafficking convictions (Pajarito, 2015).

Information and resources are leveraged and shared among relevant actors.

Cases of trafficking and corruption are often dealt with separately. According to the United Nations Office on Drugs and Crime (UNODC), there is a lack of referral to the relevant authorities of: 1) cases of trafficking in persons where there are indicators for corruption; and 2) referral of corruption cases where there are indicators of trafficking in persons. Co-operation is therefore essential among relevant actors to share information and resources. This can be done through the establishment of taskforces or joint operations. It is also crucial to establish protocols between non-governmental organisations (NGOs) and law enforcement bodies to co-ordinate their activities so that both sides understand and acknowledge the efforts and responsibilities of the other.

Furthermore, anti-money laundering systems can be used to detect and prevent the financing of trafficking in persons, and assist in the confiscation of profits from trafficking in persons as well as the prevention of the reinvestment of illicit funds into the criminal trafficking networks. Financial intelligence systems that are already in place can be used to map the activities of trafficking networks and how these networks interact with corrupt officials.

From the outset, the Philippines adopted a multi-disciplinary approach to the work against trafficking in persons with the establishment of an Inter-Agency Council Against Trafficking (IACAT) composed of 13 government agencies and 3 NGOs. In addition to the numerous functions IACAT has been tasked to perform under the "Anti-Trafficking in Persons Act", its duties also include co-ordinating the work of the various member agencies and co-ordinating awareness-raising and outreach activities. Representatives from government agencies and civil society alike reported that IACAT has been successful in its work. However, what is missing in the membership of IACAT is the inclusion of government agencies in charge of anti-corruption policies and anti-corruption enforcement in the public sector. Considering the link between trafficking in persons and corruption, one suggestion that was highlighted during the consultations conducted on the Guiding Principles was to amend the "Expanded Anti-Trafficking in Persons Act (R.A. 10364)" to include the Office of the Ombudsman in the list of members of IACAT so that information and expertise on corruption and its link to trafficking could be shared. This would also facilitate the dissemination of best practices and lessons learned from the anti-corruption field that could be included in the work conducted in the fight against trafficking in persons.

Although there are numerous examples of cross-agency co-operation and co-ordination, representatives from the non-governmental sector highlighted in interviews with the OECD that, when it comes to data collection, there is still not a functioning shared database in place. Law enforcement continues in part to work in silos, and with the porous borders of the Philippines, this means that criminal elements are able to slip through. Moving forward, it is therefore recommended that more effort is devoted to facilitating the sharing of information between concerned agencies and that data available is collected in a joint database. This will be further elaborated on under the heading "Improvement of Data Collection and Systematic Use of Information" below.

Corruption is also investigated when investigating trafficking in persons.

According to the Council of Europe, investigations and prosecutions of trafficking in persons should be accompanied by investigations into corruption and finances of suspects. In order to effectively deal with trafficking-in-persons-related corruption, indicators need to be developed for actors working in the field of trafficking in persons to detect corruption when investigating trafficking cases.

In relation to victim interviews, there were no reports of any specific interview questions that relate to government officials' involvement in the trafficking process. However, representatives from NGOs highlighted that if any information about a public official's involvement comes up during the interview they conduct in the shelters they manage, this is reported to the relevant agencies. This is an area where improvements could be made – for example, by including specific questions on public officials' involvement in standardised interview templates or by integrating a mechanism for documenting corruption allegations in NGOs' case management systems.

Specialised multi-agency units are established and multi-agency trainings are organised.

At the national level, countries could enhance co-operation between anti-corruption and anti-trafficking practitioners, for example through multi-agency training and specialised multi-agency units staffed by prosecutors and selected police.

IACAT has created a number of taskforces, among which six are port-based, inter-agency anti-trafficking taskforces. For example, if one of these port-based, inter-agency anti-trafficking taskforces is located in a sea port, it would be composed of – among others – prosecutors, social workers, port police, the navy and the coast guard. The creation of joint taskforces has been reported by government representative as a best practice in the case of the Philippines' work against trafficking in persons.

Although there are several examples of multi-agency trainings being organised on the topic of trafficking in persons, there is a need for an increased involvement of anti-corruption stakeholders in these initiatives. This is a suggestion for improvement moving forward.

3. Transparency and an integrity framework for public officials at risk

Specific rules/standards of behaviour – such as guidelines or codes of conduct – with respect to corruption and trafficking for public officials at risk are in place. The violations of the codes of conduct entail sanctions.

The conduct of the international peacekeepers, civilian police, intergovernmental and non-governmental organisations' staff and diplomatic personnel has raised serious concerns in relation to trafficking in persons and corruption. According to the cases analysed by the Council of Europe, the problem is reported to be particularly widespread among the police. One way of addressing this can be to include specific rules/standards of behaviour with respect to corruption and trafficking, for example, in codes of conduct. As supervision, discipline, and accountability are key in preventing and combating corruption, effective mechanisms are needed for reporting, investigating and sanctioning the violation of these codes of conduct for officials at risk.

Many of the sectors of public officials that could play a role in trafficking in persons are already covered by codes of conduct. However, some of these codes may need to be updated in order to address the specific issues relating to trafficking in persons. UNODC has proposed a number of specific measures that countries can implement, for example, requesting police staff who are conducting brothel raids to always be accompanied by one or more colleagues, preferably female staff, when conducting raids in brothels.

Section 7 of "Republic Act No. 6713" that establishes a Code of Conduct and "Ethical Standards for Public Officials and Employees" establishes a number of unlawful acts, such as directly or indirectly having any financial or material interest in any transaction requiring the approval of their office; own, control, manage or accept employment in any private enterprise regulated, supervised or licensed by their office unless expressly allowed by law; engage in the private practice of their profession unless authorised by the Constitution or law, provided, that such practice will not conflict or tend to conflict with their official functions; recommend any person to any position in a private enterprise which has a regular or pending official transaction with their office; using or divulging, confidential or classified information officially known to them by reason of their office and not made available to the public to further their private interests, give undue advantage to anyone; or to prejudice the public interest; or solicit or accept gifts. Violations of Sections 7 (Prohibited Acts and Transactions), 8 (Statements and Disclosure) or 9 (Divestment) of the Act is punishable with imprisonment not exceeding five years, or a fine not exceeding PHP 5 000, or both, and, in the discretion of the court of competent jurisdiction, disqualification to hold public office.

Except for the broad legal requirements listed above, interviewed stakeholders did not report on any rules, standards of conduct or specific measures that address the link between human trafficking and corruption. However, there have previously been initiatives aimed at introducing these sorts of measures – such as, for example, the "Handbook on Vulnerabilities of Government Agencies to Corruption and Complicity in Human Trafficking" that was produced by the Visayan Forum Foundation and Ateneo de Manila University. It is suggested that government agencies consider introducing rules or standards of conduct on trafficking-in-persons-related corruption in the future.

The activities of staff working in sectors at risk are performed in a transparent manner.

Sectors at specific risk of corruption in the trafficking-in-persons context need to ensure that their staff's activities are performed in a transparent manner and that unnecessary bureaucracy is eliminated so that the opportunities for corrupt officials to seek bribes are limited. This is particularly relevant within law enforcement (e.g. border control, customs and immigration authorities) and criminal justice authorities. As raised by UNODC, ensuring that the staff's activities are performed in a transparent manner does not necessarily mean public disclosure of assets and private interests but rather safeguards, such as for example internal approval systems of tasks to be performed and avoiding having one-to-one meetings with individuals, such as visa and work permit applicants, presumed trafficking victims and suspects. In addition, independent legal audit of trafficking cases could be conducted in order to assure that cases were handled in a correct manner.

Except for the legal requirement in "Republic Act No. 6713" that public officials and employees in general should "provide information of their policies and procedures in clear and understandable language, ensure openness of information, public consultations and hearings whenever appropriate, encourage suggestions, simplify and systematise policy, rules and procedures, [and] avoid red tape", there were no reports during the consultations in Manila with representatives from different government agencies and non-governmental organisations on any specific initiatives that aimed at increasing the transparency of public officials' activities in relation to trafficking. This is especially relevant within the law enforcement and criminal justice authorities that are at particular risk of trafficking-in-persons-related corruption. Moving forward, it is recommended that safeguards and initiatives specifically targeted at these public officials are introduced. In addition, interviewed stakeholders suggested that independent legal audits of trafficking cases could be introduced in order to assure that cases were handled in a correct manner. These independent audits could look into issues such as why cases were dismissed, and if any weaknesses identified were linked to corruption or undue influence.

A wider framework of integrity for public officials is promoted.

In addition to establishing rules/standards on the behaviour of public officials in respect to corruption and trafficking, countries can benefit from promoting a wider framework ensuring the integrity of public officials, including: asset disclosure regime; conflict-of-interest legislation; and whistleblower protection. Of particular focus are issues such as outside positions for police officers (for example when police officers take up positions as security guards for bars and clubs). Officials at risk should also receive general anti-corruption training that could contribute to the prevention and combating of corruption in trafficking in persons. These need to be context specific and address potential issues such as cultures of corruption and gift-giving.

Asset and liabilities disclosure, outside employment and conflicts of interest are all regulated by law in the Philippines. The "Anti-Graft and Corrupt Practices Act (R.A. 3019)" (Republic of the Philippines, 1960) requires in Section 7 that all public officers must submit a statement of assets and liabilities upon taking office, every year during his time in office, and upon the expiration of his office or his resignation. This requirement is also stated – albeit in slightly different wording – in "Republic Act 6713" that establishes a "Code of Conduct and Ethical Standards for Public Officials and Employees". "Republic Act 6713" also regulates outside employment, stating in Section 7(b) that "Public officials and employees during their incumbency shall not: 1) own, control, manage or accept employment as an officer, employee, consultant, counsel, broker, agent, trustee or nominee in any private enterprise regulated, supervised or licensed by their office unless expressly allowed by law; 2) engage in the private practice of their profession unless authorized by the Constitution or law, provided, that such practice will not conflict or tend to conflict with their official functions; or 3) recommend any person to any position in a private enterprise that has a regular or pending official transaction with their office." In relation to conflicts of interest, the "Anti-Graft and Corrupt Practices Act" makes it unlawful to "[d]irectly or indirectly having financial or pecuniary interest in any business, contract or transaction in connection with which he intervenes or takes part in his official capacity, or in which he is prohibited by the Constitution or by any law from having any interest" (Section 3[h]) or "[d]irectly or indirectly becoming interested, for personal gain, or having a material interest in any transaction or act requiring the approval of a board, panel or group of which he is a member, and which exercises discretion in such approval, even if he votes against the same or does not participate in the action of the board, committee, panel or group" (Section 3[i]).

There is no whistleblower protection act in the Philippines. An act granting protection, security and benefits to whistleblowers has been discussed for years,[1] but so far, it has not been passed in the Senate. Representatives from government agencies and non-governmental organisations alike highlighted that a law on this would make a substantial difference in their everyday work. For now, there are examples of whistleblower policies in place in a number of ministries. However, as these are not supported or required by law, their enforcement depends solely on the respective ministries that introduced them. In the absence of a whistleblower protection act, protection is only afforded to witnesses under the "Witness Protection, Security and Benefit Act (R.A. 6981)" (Republic of the Philippines, 1991b) and Section 17 of the "Ombudsman Act of 1989 (R.A. 6770)" (Republic of the Philippines, 1989b).

Mechanisms that allow for public officials as well as the public to expose misconduct and report dishonest or illegal activity and that ensure the effective protection from retaliation are in place.

Confidential hotlines or similar measures for whistleblowers may be established so that public officials or private sector employees that witness corrupt behaviour by their colleagues can provide information about these activities. This can be established within government organisations as well as international organisations. Members of the public may also be given clear channels for exposing misconduct and reporting dishonest or illegal activity occurring in public and private sector organisations. Countries need to ensure that whistleblowers are effectively protected from retaliation and intimidation.

Although there is no whistleblower protection act in the Philippines, there is an online platform established called "IDULOG" where it is possible to file complaints against frontline agencies.[2] Representatives from the non-governmental sector who were interviewed for this report stated that although this "catch all" platform is a good initiative, a web platform will mainly be used in urban areas, which means that it is only reaching a limited proportion of the population. In addition to IDULOG, it is also possible to file complaints on line with the Office of the Ombudsman, or call the OMB hotline.

Moving forward, it is essential that steps are taken to ensure that whistleblowers are effectively protected from retaliation and intimidation. As previously highlighted, there is no whistleblower protection act in place in the Philippines.

The recruitment process of officials is transparent, competitive and subject to independent scrutiny. Upon recruitment, officials receive training, adequate supervision and are subject to regular performance evaluations.

Recruitment of key officials, in particular those employed in anti-corruption or anti-trafficking units, prosecutors and judicial officials needs to consistently be conducted by the means of a transparent and competitive selection process that is subject to independent scrutiny. Upon recruitment, key officials would benefit from receiving training, adequate supervision and be subject to regular performance evaluations. It is important that the training does not only cover instructions relating to specific tasks and responsibilities that the employee will encounter, but also the standards of conduct and values of the organisation.

Regarding the taskforces set up by IACAT, there is no public information on how the recruitment or selection of participants takes place. In interviews conducted with the IACAT Secretariat, it was reported that they were vetted and selected based on their integrity and expertise. Moving forward, it is recommended that the procedures and selection criteria are formalised and communicated to the public, so that it is possible for stakeholders to assist in the monitoring of the process. The same holds true for methods of supervision and performance evaluations.

In relation to the general recruitment processes of public officials, civil society stakeholders indicated that there is still work to be done in order to ensure that processes of hiring and promotion are based solely on merit. It was reported that patronage ties still has a strong influence and importance in the process, with for example, letters of recommendation from high-ranking, elected officials having great influence in qualifying for promotion or hiring.

Key officials receive training so that they are able to correctly identify trafficking victims, understand the nature of the crime, and recognise warning signs throughout the different stages of the trafficking-in-persons process.

In order to correctly identify and deal with trafficking-in-persons cases, it is essential that key officials receive training. Experience shows that the first government official a victim of trafficking is likely to meet is a local police officer and not a lawmaker or diplomat, and if this local police officer has not been trained to identify trafficking victims and understand the crime, there is a heightened risk that the crime is not properly identified. Also, for example, consular staff in countries of origin may benefit from exchanging experiences and being trained in recognising visa applications that could involve trafficking in persons.

In 2014, the Philippine Overseas Employment Agency (POEA) conducted 13 seminars on the expanded anti-trafficking law (US Department of State, 2015). In the past four years, POEA also conducted 157 Anti-Illegal Recruitment/Trafficking-in-Persons Seminars that reached 13 111 participants across the country. In the most recent data available, 90% of the participants in these seminars were prosecutors, local government personnel, law enforcement officers, and Public Service Employment Office employees (United Nations, 2013). The government also provided anti-trafficking training or guidance to its diplomatic personnel and Philippine troops prior to their deployment abroad (US Department of State, 2015).

According to the US Department of State (2015), IACAT and its taskforces conducted 99 trainings and workshops on trafficking in persons, reaching more than 5 000 prosecutors, law enforcers and social workers in 2014.

Several of the stakeholders from both government agencies and non-governmental organisations that were interviewed for this report stated that more trainings were needed for law enforcement officers. Trainings were suggested to deal with the collection of evidence, as minor missteps can make the information collected inadmissible in court. There were also suggestions that more trainings should be conducted for first responders so that they are able to correctly identify the crime as falling under the "Trafficking in Persons Act". Although some work has been done on this in relation to sex trafficking, there was a call for more trainings that focus on how to identify trafficking in labour cases. If done correctly, it was argued that this could increase the number of prosecutions on forced labour in the Philippines.

Moving forward, it is recommended that the Philippines continues to strengthen its trainings to key officials so that they are able to correctly identify trafficking victims, understand the nature of the crime, and recognise warning signs throughout the different stages of the trafficking-in-persons process.

4. *Awareness-raising and prevention measures for public officials and the general public*

Public awareness regarding the existence, causes, and gravity of trafficking in persons and the active participation of individuals and groups outside the public sector in the prevention of and the fight against trafficking-in-persons-related corruption is promoted.

Article 13 of the United Nations Convention against Corruption (UNCAC) (United Nations, 2003) demands that each State Party shall take the appropriate measures to promote the "active participation of individuals and groups outside the public sector, such as civil society, non-governmental organisations and community-based organisations, in the prevention of, and the fight against, corruption and to raise public awareness regarding the existence, causes and gravity of, and the threat posed by, corruption." Specific measures to strengthen this participation include:

1. enhancing the transparency of and promoting the contribution of the public to decision-making processes
2. ensuring that the public has effective access to information
3. undertaking public information activities that contribute to non-tolerance of corruption, as well as public education programmes, including school and university curricula
4. respecting, promoting and protecting the freedom to seek, receive, publish and disseminate information concerning corruption.

Similarly, Article 9(2) of the United Nations "Protocol to Prevent, Suppress and Punish Trafficking in Persons, Especially Women and Children", establishes that State Parties shall "endeavour to undertake measures such as research, information and mass media campaigns and social and economic initiatives to prevent and combat trafficking in persons." The Council of Europe suggests giving particular attention to the development of special awareness programmes in schools.

In order to effectively raise awareness of the linkages between corruption and trafficking in persons, countries can involve and train media and facilitate investigative journalism on trafficking in persons and corruption. Furthermore, media can play an important role in increasing public awareness and knowledge on TIP and corruption hotspots, deterring offenders by highlighting arrests and prosecutions, and rewarding and encouraging successful law enforcement through the publication of success stories.

According to the US Department of State, "[a]uthorities allocated PHP 200 000 (USD 4 500) for community education programmes on trafficking in nine provinces, which reached more than 2 500 participants, including prospective migrants" (2015, p. 281). They also report that the Department of Social Welfare and Development conducted 54 advocacy activities on the anti-trafficking law that reached over 2 000 people across the Philippines. In addition, IACAT funded anti-trafficking forums and orientation workshops for approximately 10 000 students, women and children's rights advocates, and the Philippine National Police conducted 6 138 community activities to discuss enforcement of the anti-trafficking in persons law (US Department of State, 2015). POEA produced Anti-Illegal Recruitment videos that were viewed 217 742 times, and disseminated 528 750 printed materials in 2014 (Larga, 2015).

The government also made significant efforts to reach out to the public through social media, radio and television. Examples include IACAT and POEA Facebook pages and Twitter accounts,[3] IACAT's YouTube channel,[4] and the weekly public awareness radio programme on 702 DZAS AM.[5]

In regards to participation, there are three NGO members representing women, overseas Filipinos, and children, on the Inter-Agency Council Against Trafficking. They are appointed for a term of three years. This gives NGOs an opportunity to bring their unique perspective and serve as a watchdog in ensuring that IACAT does what it is mandated to do. Given the close co-operation between government agencies and NGOs and some NGOs' reliance on government funding, it could however be questioned if they can speak freely without fear of repercussions.

Non-governmental organisations interviewed by the OECD in August 2015 highlighted that there is a need for more outreach to the younger generation on anti-corruption and integrity. Suggestions included organising meetings between youth and local government officials recognised for their integrity, thereby introducing role models for those interested in careers in the public service.

Targeted awareness-raising measures for all parties involved in anti-trafficking issues are provided.

In addition to general anti-corruption measures, specific awareness raising measures that highlight vulnerabilities, responsibilities, risks, and draw attention to how corrupt behaviour could facilitate the crime of trafficking in persons and the re-victimisation of the trafficked victims are essential to understand the links and forms of trafficking. Consequently, these measures need to be provided for all parties involved in anti-trafficking issues, including police and anti-trafficking organisations.

In the OECD interviews conducted with government agencies and representatives from civil society in August 2015, there were few reports of specific awareness-raising measures that focused on how corrupt behaviour could facilitate the crime of trafficking except for the trainings that were highlighted above. Moving forward, there is a need for the issues of corruption and human trafficking to be better integrated in the different awareness-raising initiatives being implemented by the Filipino government.

Preventive measures for potential victims of trafficking in persons are in place, in particular offering counselling about corruption and trafficking before and after they have undertaken a migration journey and alerting communities of early signs of corruption.

It is essential to build civic response and community awareness about the linkages between corruption and trafficking in persons. Specific measures proposed by the UNODC for potential victims of trafficking include: 1) alerting communities that early signs of corruption in a legitimate migration journey should be considered as warning indicators that trafficking may be taking place; and 2) giving citizens access to free, confidential counselling about corruption and trafficking before and after they have undertaken a migration journey, in order to make them aware of their rights and capable of looking for help if they are infringed in a way that renders them victims of trafficking.

One example of an agency that has invested resources in preventive measures is the Philippine Overseas Employment Agency (POEA). POEA conducts Pre-Employment

Orientation Seminars (PEOS), where workers that are about to go abroad are informed of the laws in their country of destination and precautionary measures against illegal recruitment. These seminars will in the near future become a mandatory requirement before going abroad. POEA has so far reached about 1.33 million participants, with more than 500 000 of these in 2014 alone. The eight modules are also available on line for those who are not near a location where the seminars are given.[6] So far, PEOS online has received 285 850 visits.[7] POEA has also developed a PEOS mobile application where it is possible to verify if the employment agency that a future migrant worker is considering is licensed, and if the agency's license is suspended or not. The availability of a job being offered by the agency can also be checked in this mobile application. If it is not listed on line, there is a risk that the job offer the prospective migrant worker has received is fictitious. Between March 2014 and August 2015, there were 90 000 downloads of the PEOS mobile application. It can be downloaded for free. There were no reports of any specific anti-corruption or corruption-awareness components included in the trainings. This could be an addition moving forward.

In addition to the prevention measures implemented by the POEA, there are a number of other public awareness initiatives under way in the Philippines, such as IACAT's television show promoting trafficking awareness, the distribution of printed materials and information made available on social media.[8] There are also numerous initiatives from civil society that have worked proactively with the education and outreach in at-risk communities. This includes the iFIGHT Movement by the Visayan Forum Foundation that through awareness-raising in partnership with schools and universities in the Philippines aims at preventing human trafficking. These various examples are further elaborated on under the Guiding Principle on Public awareness regarding the existence, causes, and gravity of trafficking in person, above.

5. Improvement of data collection and systematic use of information

Data on trafficking in persons are collected, analysed and used systematically.

Most countries are not systematically collecting and analysing data on investigations or prosecutions of public officials relating to trafficking in persons and corruption. There are many reasons for the scarcity of data. Among the most important reasons highlighted by the International Organization for Migration (IOM) are the victims' reluctance to report or testify for fear of reprisals; lack of harmonisation among existing data sources; and the opposition of some countries and agencies to share data. As a crucial step in addressing trafficking-in-persons-related corruption, countries need to focus on the collection of data and information in order to get a better insight into the problem. Because of its transnational nature, data on trafficking-in-persons-related corruption also needs to be collected and aggregated at the regional level. It should be stressed that any legal provisions or policy decisions on data collection and/or the creation of databases need to be accompanied by a commitment of resources for implementation.

Information on corruption provided by victims and NGOs can also be used more systematically. Government agencies working on anti-corruption and anti-trafficking need to co-operate with the non-governmental sector and civil society to ensure that information and experiences from victims are collected (through, for example, interviews) and that this information is passed on to the anti-corruption and anti-trafficking units in government. By improving the data collection and systemic use of information, countries would be allowed to implement targeted responses based on facts.

The "Expanded Anti-Trafficking in Persons Act of 2012 (R.A. 10364)" stipulates that a central anti-trafficking in persons database should be established by the Inter-Agency

Council Against Trafficking (IACAT). The Act also requires all government agencies that are tasked with working on trafficking in persons to submit the data they have to the Council for integration into the central database. As a minimum, the database has to include information on the number of cases of trafficking in persons sorted according to the status of cases (including the number of cases being investigated, submitted for prosecution, dropped, and filed and/or pending before the courts, and the number of convictions and acquittals); the number of victims of trafficking in persons referred to the agency by destination countries/areas and by area of origin; and disaggregated data on trafficking victims and the accused/defendants.

The data that is made available at IACAT's website includes only the date and location of the crime, number of convictions, number persons of convicted, the acts committed as defined by the "Anti-Trafficking in Persons Act", number of years of imprisonment and the amount of the fines (IACAT, 2015b). This means that requirements such as information on the number of cases being investigated, submitted for prosecution, dropped, and filed and/or pending before the courts are either not collected, or if collected, not made publicly available. This makes it difficult to track progress of cases, and to bring attention to cases that have been dropped that could warrant further investigations into the reason for dropping them. Stakeholders have also argued that information on employers of trafficking victims should be made available in the database.

Representatives from the non-governmental sector stated in interviews with the OECD that when it comes to data collection, there is still not a functioning shared database in place. When law enforcement agencies are not co-operating with each other, criminal elements are able to slip through and cross the porous borders of the Philippines. Moving forward, it is therefore recommended that more effort is devoted to facilitating the sharing of information between concerned agencies and that data available is collected in a joint database.

On the topic of TIP-related corruption, government representatives stated that although data on administrative sanctions against public officials probably is available within each ministry, there have been no attempts to aggregate this information at the national level. In relation to administrative sanctions related to TIP, interviewed government officials stated that it was unlikely that this data was available for all government agencies.

Moving forward, it is recommended that data is made available on the number of filed and investigated cases, and not only the number of convictions. Also, it would be valuable to include information on why cases were dropped as this would be a way to identify red flags of potential corruption in the process. In relation to administrative and criminal sanctions, it is recommended that data on the number of investigated and prosecuted government officials in relation to trafficking in persons is extractable from the database.

6. Lift immunity in corruption and trafficking cases

Immunity from prosecution of public officials is duly lifted to allow for effective investigation, prosecution and adjudication of corruption and trafficking-in-persons-related offences.

The purpose of immunity is to protect the independence of public officials and make sure that they will make difficult decisions without risking facing personal consequences for this decision (e.g. being sued). According to UNCAC Article 30(2), "Each State Party shall take such measures as may be necessary to establish or maintain, in accordance with its legal system and constitutional principles, an appropriate balance between any immunities or jurisdictional privileges accorded to its public officials for the performance of their functions and the possibility, when necessary, of effectively investigating, prosecuting and adjudicating offences established in accordance with this Convention." Similarly, in cases of trafficking in persons, countries need to lift the immunity from prosecution of public officials following an allegation of corruption that is supported by evidence.

The "Expanded Anti-Trafficking in Persons Act of 2012 (R.A. 10364)" introduces the following section into the "Anti-Trafficking in Persons Act of 2003 (R.A. 9208)":

> *Immunity from Suit, Prohibited Acts and Injunctive Remedies.* – No action or suit shall be brought, instituted or maintained in any court or tribunal or before any other authority against any: (a) law enforcement officer; (b) social worker; or (c) person acting in compliance with a lawful order from any of the above, for lawful acts done or statements made during an authorized rescue operation, recovery or rehabilitation/intervention, or an investigation or prosecution of an anti-trafficking case: *Provided,* That such acts shall have been made in good faith.

The law therefore only grants immunity to law enforcement officers, social workers, or others acting in compliance with a lawful order from law enforcement officers or social workers, if the acts committed were lawful and made in good faith. If this is not the case, Section 12 of the "Expanded Anti-Trafficking Act of 2012" that amends Section 10 of "Republic Act No. 9208" establishes:

- a penalty of 15 years in prison and a fine of PHP 500 000 to PHP 1 million to anyone who 1) tampers or causes the destruction of evidence or influences or attempts to influence witnesses in an investigation or prosecution; or 2) utilises his or her office to impede investigation, prosecution or execution of lawful order.
- a penalty of life in prison and a fine between PHP 2 million and PHP 5 million to anyone who commits qualified trafficking, which, for example, is the case if the offender is a member of the military or law enforcement agencies.

In addition, Section 12 of the "Expanded Anti-Trafficking in Persons Act of 2012" that amends Section 10(j) of "Republic Act No. 9208" stipulates that "[a]ny employee or official of government agencies who shall issue or approve the issuance of travel exit clearances, passports, registration certificates, counselling certificates, marriage licenses, and other similar documents to persons, whether juridical or natural, recruitment agencies, establishments or other individuals or groups, who fail to observe the prescribed procedures and the requirement as provided for by laws, rules and regulations, shall be held administratively liable, without prejudice to criminal liability under this Act. The concerned government official or employee shall, upon conviction, be dismissed from the service and be barred permanently to hold public office. His or her retirement and other benefits shall likewise be forfeited." Finally, Section 13 that amends Section 11 addresses the demand side of trafficking. Also, if the offender is a public official, the Act stipulates that "he or she shall be dismissed from service and shall suffer perpetual absolute disqualification to hold public office, in addition to any imprisonment or fine received pursuant to any other provision of this Act" (Section 10[j]).

Stakeholders' feedback on the Guiding Principles and findings from the in-country testing

The "Guiding Principles on Combatting Corruption related to Trafficking in Persons" were well received by government agencies and civil society actors alike. Areas highlighted as particularly relevant included the Guiding Principles' joint focus on trafficking and corruption – an area that stakeholders believed required further work in the case of the Philippines – and the need for trainings and education on the laws in place so that crimes are correctly identified and public officials know what is expected of them. Suggestions from consulted stakeholders on additional points that could be incorporated, based on their experiences from the Philippines, include:

- a strong focus on the importance of implementation, as good laws on paper will not be enough in addressing trafficking in persons and corruption
- addressing the problems associated with a deeply rooted culture of gift-giving, favours, and money changing hands when formulating and implementing anti-corruption laws and measures
- addressing the importance of ensuring that there is sufficient political will at all levels of government in addressing TIP-related corruption, including at the local level
- introducing independent legal audits of trafficking cases in order to ensure that cases were handled in a correct manner
- highlighting the importance of leadership in putting the issues of trafficking in persons and corruption on the national agenda.

Regarding the principle on "Improvement of Data Collection and Systematic Use of Information", stakeholders highlighted that it is not enough to mandate the creation of a shared database in the law. There also needs to be a commitment of resources attached to the implementation of the provision.

The testing of the Guiding Principles in the Philippines showed that they not only reflect many of the good practices that country representatives highlighted, but that they also raise recommendations in areas where more work is needed to effectively address trafficking-in-persons-related corruption.

Notes

1. See, for example, Senate of the Philippines (2013), "An Act Providing for the Protection, Security and Benefits of Whistleblowers, Appropriating Funds Therefor and for Other Purposes", Senate Bill No. 1932, www.senate.gov.ph/lisdata/1825515452!.pdf and Senate of the Philippines (2009), "An Act Providing for Whistleblower Bill of Rights", Senate Bill No. 3533, www.senate.gov.ph/lisdata/1301611690!.pdf.

2. Available at www.gov.ph/feedback/idulog/.

3. Available at www.facebook.com/IACAT.NEWS, twitter.com/iacatnews, www.facebook.com/mypoea and twitter.com/poeaNews.

4 Available at www.youtube.com/user/iacatnews/videos.

5. Live streamed at www.febc.ph.

6. See http://peos.poea.gov.ph/index.php/peos/dashboard.

7. As of August 2015.

8. See, for example: www.facebook.com/IACAT.NEWS, twitter.com/iacatnews and www.youtube.com/user/iacatnews/videos.

References

ASEAN (Association of Southeast Asian Nations) (2010), *ASEAN Handbook on International Legal Cooperation in Trafficking in Persons Cases*, ASEAN Secretariat, Jakarta, www.unodc.org/documents/human-trafficking/ASEAN_Handbook_on_International_Legal_Cooperation_in_TIP_Cases.pdf.

ASEAN (2004a), "ASEAN Declaration Against Trafficking in Persons Particularly Women and Children", Vientiane, 29 November, www1.umn.edu/humanrts/research/Philippines/ASEAN%20Declaration%20Against%20Trafficking%20in%20Persons%20Particularly%20Women%20and%20Children.pdf.

ASEAN (Association of Southeast Asian Nations) (2004b), "2004 Treaty on Mutual Legal Assistance in Criminal Matters", Kuala Lumpur, Malaysia, 29 November, http://cil.nus.edu.sg/rp/pdf/2004%20Treaty%20on%20Mutual%20Legal%20Assistance%20in%20Criminal%20Matters-pdf.pdf

Bureau of Immigration (2015), "Immigration Officer Instrumental in Conviction of Human Trafficking Syndicate", press release, Republic of the Philippines, www.immigration.gov.ph/faqs/index.php?option=com_content&view=article&id=795&catid=112.

Canlas, J. (2015), "Countries unite vs. human trafficking", *The Manila Times*, 8 June, www.manilatimes.net/countries-unite-vs-human-trafficking/190240/.

Guth, A. P. (2010), "Human trafficking in the Philippines: The need for an effective anti-corruption program", *Trends in Organized crime*, 13 (2), pp. 147-166.

IACAT (Inter-Agency Council Against Trafficking) (2015a), "IACAT lauds international stance against trafficking", press release, http://iacat.gov.ph/index.php/159-iacat-lauds-international-stance-against-trafficking.

IACAT (2015b), *Resources: Statistics*, database, www.iacat.net/index.php/human-trafficking-related-statistics (accessed on 2 September 2015).

IACAT (2012), "The Second National Strategic Action Plan Against Trafficking in Persons 2012-2016", IACAT/UNICEF.

ILO (International Labour Organization) (2011), "Domestic Workers Convention, 2011 (No. 189)", Geneva, 16 June, www.ilo.org/dyn/normlex/en/f?p=NORMLEXPUB:12100:0::NO::P12100_INSTRUMENT_ID:2551460.

ILO (1999), "Worst Forms of Child Labour Convention, 1999 (No. 182)", Geneva, 17 June, www.ilo.org/dyn/normlex/en/f?p=NORMLEXPUB:12100:0::NO:12100:P12100_ILO_CODE:C182.

ILO (1957), "Abolition of Forced Labour Convention, 1957 (No. 105)", ILO, Geneva, 25 June, www.ilo.org/dyn/normlex/en/f?p=1000:12100:0::NO::P12100_ILO_CODE:C105.

ILO (1930), "Forced Labour Convention, 1930 (No. 29)", Geneva, 28 June, www.ilo.org/dyn/normlex/en/f?p=NORMLEXPUB:12100:0::NO::P12100_INSTRUMENT_ID:312174.

ILO (n.d.), "Labour migration", www.ilo.org/manila/areasofwork/labour-migration/lang--en/index.htm (accessed on 15 March 2016).

Larga,R.L. (2015), "Awareness-raising and Preventive Measures Against Illegal Recruitment and Trafficking in Persons: The POEA Experience", presentation, OECD Roundtable on Combatting Corruption related to Trafficking in Persons, Cebu City, Philippines, 27 August.

Pajarito, D. (2015), "Inter-Agency Council Against Trafficking (IACAT)", presentation, OECD Roundtable on Combatting Corruption related to Trafficking in Persons, Cebu City, the Philippines, 27 August.

Republic of the Philippines (2012a), "Republic Act No. 10364: Expanded Anti-Trafficking in Persons Act of 2012", www.gov.ph/2013/02/06/republic-act-no-10364/.

Republic of the Philippines (2012b), "Republic Act No. 10365: An Act Further Strengthening the Anti-Money Laundering Law, Amending for the Purpose Republic Act No. 9160, Otherwise Known as The 'Anti-Money Laundering Act Of 2001', As Amended", www.gov.ph/2013/02/15/republic-act-no-10365/.

Republic of the Philippines (2009a), "Republic Act No. 10022: An Act Amending Republic Act No. 8042, Otherwise Known as the Migrant Workers and Overseas Filipinos Act of 1995, as Amended, Further Improving the Standard of Protection and Promotion of the Welfare of Migrant Workers, Their Families and Overseas Filipinos in Distress, and for Other Purposes", www.poea.gov.ph/ptfair/ra10022.htm.

Republic of the Philippines (2009b), "Republic Act No. 9995: An Act Defining and Penalizing the Crime of Photo and Video Voyeurism, Prescribing Penalties Therefor, and for Other Purposes", http://www.lawphil.net/statutes/repacts/ra2010/ra_9995_2010.html.

Republic of the Philippines (2009c), "Republic Act No. 9775: Anti-Child Pornography Act of 2009", http://www1.umn.edu/humanrts/research/Philippines/RA%209775%20-%20Anti-Child%20Pornography%20Act%20of%202009.pdf.

Republic of the Philippines (2003a), "Republic Act No. 9208: Anti-Trafficking in Persons Act of 2003", www.hsph.harvard.edu/population/trafficking/philippines.traf.03.htm.

Republic of the Philippines (2003b), " Republic Act No. 9231: An Act Providing for the Elimination of the Worst Forms of Child Labor and Affording Stronger Protection for the Working Child, Amending for this Purpose Republic Act No. 7610, As Amended, Otherwise Known as the 'Special Protection of Children Against Child Abuse, Exploitation And Discrimination Act'", bwsc.dole.gov.ph/images/ppacl/WCP/Republic-Act-No-9231.pdf.

Republic of the Philippines (1995a), "Republic Act No. 8043: An Act Establishing the Rules to Govern Inter-Country Adoption of Filipino Children, and for Other Purposes", http://pcw.gov.ph/law/republic-act-8043.

Republic of the Philippines (1995b),"Republic Act No. 8042: Migrant Workers and Overseas Filipinos Act of 1995", www.poea.gov.ph/rules/ra8042.html.

Republic of the Philippines (1992)," Republic Act No. 7610: An Act Providing for Stronger Deterrence and Special Protection against Child Abuse, Exploitation and Discrimination, and for Other Purposes", www.gov.ph/1992/06/17/republic-act-no-7610/.

Republic of the Philippines (1991a), "Republic Act No. 7080: An Act Defining and Penalizing the Crime of Plunder", www.dole.gov.ph/files/RA%207080.pdf.

Republic of the Philippines (1991b),"Republic Act No. 6981: An Act Providing for a Witness Protection, Security and Benefit Program and for Other Purposes", www.lawphil.net/statutes/repacts/ra1991/ra_6981_1991.html .

Republic of the Philippines (1990), "Republic Act No. 6955: An Act to Declare Unlawful the Practice of Matching Filipino Women for Marriage to Foreign Nationals on a Mail Order Basis and Other Similar Practices, Including the Advertisement, Publication, Printing or Distribution of Brochures, Fliers and Other Propaganda Materials in Furtherance Thereof and Providing Penalty Therefore", www.lawphil.net/statutes/repacts/ra1990/ra_6955_1990.html.

Republic of the Philippines (1989a), "Republic Act No. 6713: An Act Establishing a Code of Conduct and Ethical Standards for Public Officials and Employees, to Uphold the Time-Honored Principle of Public Office Being a Public Trust, Granting Incentives and Rewards for Exemplary Service, Enumerating Prohibited Acts and Transactions and Providing Penalties for Violations Thereof and for Other Purposes", www.dole.gov.ph/files/RA%206713.pdf.

Republic of the Philippines (1989b), "Republic Act No. 6770: An Act Providing for the Functional and Structural Organization of the Office of the Ombudsman, and for Other Purposes", www.ombudsman.gov.ph/docs/republicacts/Republic_Act_No_6770.pdf.

Republic of the Philippines (1972), "Presidential Decree No. 46: Making it Punishable for Public Officials and Employees to Receive, and for Private Persons to Give, Gifts on any Occasion, Including Christmas", 10 November, www.dole.gov.ph/files/PD%2046.pdf.

Republic of the Philippines (1960), "Republic Act No. 3019: Anti-Graft and Corrupt Practices Act", www.dole.gov.ph/files/RA%203019.pdf.

Republic of the Philippines (1955), "Republic Act No. 1379: An Act Declaring Forfeiture in Favor of the State any Property Found to Have Been Unlawfully Acquired By any Public Officer or Employee and Providing for the Proceedings Therefor", www.lawphil.net/statutes/repacts/ra1955/ra_1379_1955.html.

Republic of the Philippines (1930), "Republic Act No. 3815: An Act Revising the Penal Code and Other Penal Laws", www.lawphil.net/statutes/acts/act_3815_1930.html.

Senate of the Philippines (2013), "An Act Providing for the Protection, Security and Benefits of Whistleblowers, Appropriating Funds Therefor and for Other Purposes", Senate Bill No. 1932, www.senate.gov.ph/lisdata/1825515452!.pdf.

Senate of the Philippines (2009), "An Act Providing for Whistleblower Bill of Rights", Senate Bill No. 3533, www.senate.gov.ph/lisdata/1301611690!.pdf.

United Nations (2013), "Report of the Special Rapporteur on Trafficking in Persons, Especially Women and Children", Ms. Joy Ngozi Ezeilo, Addendum, Mission to the Philippines, United Nations General Assembly, Human Rights Council, 23rd session, Agenda item 3, A/HRC/23/48/Add.3.

United Nations (2003), "United Nations Convention against Corruption", *United Nations Treaty Series*, Vol. 2349, No. 42146, New York, 31 October, p. 41, https://treaties.un.org/doc/Publication/UNTS/Volume%202349/v2349.pdf.

United Nations (2000), "Protocol to Prevent, Suppress and Punish Trafficking in Persons, Especially Women and Children, supplementing the United Nations Convention against Transnational Organized Crime", *Treaty Collection*, database, https://treaties.un.org/Pages/ViewDetails.aspx?src=IND&mtdsg_no=XVIII-12-a&chapter=18&lang=en.

US Department of State (2015), *Trafficking in Persons Report July 2015*, US Department of State, Washington, DC.

US Department of State (2013), *Trafficking in Persons Report June 2013*, US Department of State, Washington, DC.

Chapter 5

Testing the Guiding Principles on Combatting Corruption related to Trafficking in Persons in Thailand

This chapter takes stock of the potential practical application of the "Guiding Principles on Combatting Corruption related to Trafficking in Persons" in the context of Thailand, and explores whether the Guiding Principles effectively address the concerns identified in relation to trafficking in persons and corruption.

With the goal of ensuring that the "Guiding Principles on Combatting Corruption related to Trafficking in Persons" (hereafter, the Guiding Principles) are both relevant and useful in addressing the real-life, practical, challenges identified on the ground in relation to trafficking in persons (TIP) and corruption, the Guiding Principles were tested in Thailand. The first part of this chapter will introduce the legal framework in place and the general situation in relation to TIP and corruption in Thailand. Noteworthy cases will be introduced. The second part of the chapter will highlight how the issues raised in the respective principles have been applied in the context of Thailand – and/or, if relevant, discuss any challenges or lessons learned in addressing the issues raised in the principles in question. This final part of the chapter will present the feedback on the Guiding Principles that was raised by stakeholders that were consulted during an OECD fact-finding mission to Bangkok in August 2015, and the findings from the in-country testing.

The legal framework

Thailand's "Anti-Trafficking in Persons Act B.E. 2551" (Kingdom of Thailand, 2008a) came into force in 2008. Chapter 1, Section 6 of the Act defines the crime of trafficking in persons as – for the purpose of exploitation – 1) procuring, buying, selling, vending, bringing from or sending to, detaining or confining, harbouring, or receiving any person, by means of the threat or use of force, abduction, fraud, deception, abuse of power, or of the giving of money or benefits to achieve the consent of a person having control over another person in allowing the offender to exploit the person under his control; or 2) procuring, buying, selling, vending, bringing from or sending to, detaining or confining, harbouring, or receiving a child (under the age of 18).

Section 52 of the "Anti-Trafficking in Persons Act B.E. 2551" stipulates that the penalties for anyone who "commits an offence of trafficking in persons shall be liable to the punishment of an imprisonment from four years to ten years and a fine from THB 80 000 to THB 200 000". If the offence is committed against a child who is older than 15 but has not yet turned 18, the punishment ranges from 6 to 12 years in prison and a fine between THB 120 000 and THB 240 000. If the offence is committed against a child who is younger than 15, the punishment ranges from 8 to 15 years in prison and a fine between THB 160 000 and THB 300 000.

Section 7 of the Act also stipulates a number of additional acts that are to be punished "likewise as the offender of an offence of trafficking in persons". These acts are:

1. supporting the commission of an offence of trafficking in persons
2. aiding by contributing property, procuring a meeting place or lodge, for the offender of trafficking in persons
3. assisting by any means so that the offender of trafficking in persons may not be arrested
4. demanding, accepting, or agreeing to accept a property or any other benefit in order to help the offender of trafficking in persons not to be punished
5. inducing, suggesting or contacting a person to become a member of the organised criminal group, for the purpose of committing an offence of trafficking in persons.

A number of the listed acts can be linked to the involvement of corrupt public officials – such as, for example, law enforcement officers – in the trafficking-in-persons chain. Examples include those listed in Section 7 Paragraph 3 (assisting by any means so that the offender of trafficking in persons may not be arrested) and Paragraph 4 (demanding, accepting, or agreeing to accept a property or any other benefit in order to help the offender of trafficking in persons not to be punished). Section 13 lists categories of public officials that are liable to twice the punishment for committing an offence under the Act. These include members of the House of Representatives, members of the Senate, members of a Local Administration Council, local administrators, government officials, employees of the Local Administration Organisation, or employees of an organisation or a public agency, members of a board, executives, or employees of state enterprise, officials, or members of a board of any organisation under the Constitution. If the person is a member of the Committee, member of Sub-Committee, or a member of any working group and competent official empowered to act in accordance with the Act, the punishment for committing an offence under the Act is three times the punishment stipulated for such an offence.

In addition to the "Anti-Trafficking in Persons Act" in place, Thailand has a "National Policy Strategy on Human Trafficking for 2011-16" that is operationalised through annual action plans.

In relation to corruption, Section 149 of the "Criminal Code" of Thailand (Kingdom of Thailand, 1956) stipulates that if an "official, member of the State Legislative Assembly, member of the Changwat Assembly or member of the Municipal Assembly, wrongfully demands, accepts or agrees to accept for himself or the other person a property or any other benefit for exercising or not exercising any of his functions, whether such exercise or non-exercise of his functions is wrongful or not, shall be punished with imprisonment of 5-20 years or imprisonment for life, and fined THB 2 000 to THB 40 000, or death." Section 157 of the same Act also stipulates that if any official wrongfully executes or omits to execute his or her duty with intent to cause damage to any person, or dishonestly executes or omits to execute his or her duty shall be liable to imprisonment from one year to ten years or a fine of THB 2 000 to THB 20 000, or both.

Thailand has recently enacted laws that address one of the most at-risk sectors of human trafficking in the country, namely the fishery sector. This was done partly in response to the downgrade to Tier 3 in the US *Trafficking in Persons Report*, and the European Commission's issuance of a yellow card – or in other words the issuance of a formal notice – to Thailand for not taking sufficient measures in the international fight against illegal fishing. If Thailand is not able to address its shortcomings in its fisheries monitoring, control and sanctioning systems, the European Union could ban fisheries imports from Thailand (European Commission, 2015). The newly enacted laws include the "Fishery Act B.E. 2558" (Kingdom of Thailand, 2015), the Ministry of Labour's "Regulation to Protect Labour in the Sea Fishing Industry B.E. 2557" (Kingdom of Thailand, 2014a), and the Marine Department's "Regulation on Criteria for Permission to Work in Fishing Vessels of 30 Gross Tonnage Capacity or over B.E. 2557" (Kingdom of Thailand, 2014b). As an example, the Ministry of Labour's "Regulation to Protect Labour in the Sea Fishing Industry B.E. 2557" stipulates a minimum age of 18 years for workers on sea vessels; a minimum rest period of at least ten hours; a labour contract signed with the consent of both parties; and 30 days minimum annual leave (Seafish, 2015; MSDHS, 2015). Furthermore, the Thai government is requiring fishing vessels owners to submit lists of their crews and register them at One Stop Service Centres in 22 coastal provinces (MSDHS, 2015). Joint inspections are carried out by the Department of Fisheries, the Marine Department, the Marine Police Division and the Royal Thai Navy, Department of Labour Protection and Welfare, and the Department of Employment. Some

456 inspections were reported to have been carried out between October 2014 and September 2015 (Prompoj, 2015).

The situation in Thailand

In 2014, Thailand was automatically downgraded from a Tier 2 Watch List ranking to Tier 3 in the US *Trafficking in Persons Report*, and remained at Tier 3 in the 2015 *Trafficking in Persons Report*. A Tier 3 ranking means that the government does not fully comply with the minimum standards for the elimination of trafficking, and is not making significant efforts to do so. The US *Trafficking in Persons Report* describes Thailand as a source, destination, and transit country for men, women, and children subjected to forced labour and sex trafficking (US Department of State, 2015). Labour trafficking is reported to primarily take place within commercial fishing, fishing-related industries, factories, and domestic work. The Royal Thai Police has organised its work on suppressing trafficking in persons under four pillars: prostitution; street begging; illegal labour; and Rohingya. The case of Rohingya and the current ongoing investigations against corrupt officials are elaborated on in Box 5.1.

It has been argued that Thailand provides a clear example of how corruption and human trafficking are strongly inter-related (Sakdiyakorn and Vichitrananda, 2010). The US State Department (2015) reports that although Thailand investigated and prosecuted some cases in 2014 against corrupt officials involved in trafficking, corruption continues to impede progress in combating trafficking. As an example of the link between corruption and trafficking in Thailand, Transparency International argues that Thai border officials are in a position of extreme power and would be able to block or stop the trafficking chain. However, this position of power can be leveraged for their own private benefit – as well as that of the trafficker – if they are corrupt (Transparency International, 2011). Malinvisa Sakdiyakorn and Sutthana Vichitrananda (2010) state that the forms of corruption that take place along the borders include bribery, but also directly partnering with traffickers or leading trafficking operations. Similar examples of officials' involvement are reported in the 2015 US *Trafficking in Persons Report*, where it is stated that "[m]edia sources in 2013 reported corrupt Thai civilian and military officials profited from selling Rohingya asylum seekers from Burma and Bangladesh into forced labor on fishing vessels" and that "[c]redible reports indicate some corrupt officials protect brothels and other commercial sex venues from raids and inspections; collude with traffickers; use information from victim interviews to weaken cases; and engage in commercial sex acts with child trafficking victims" (US Department of State, 2015, p. 331). According to one study, "brothels pay monthly allotments to the police for protection and in some cases the brothels are actually owned by government, military or police officials" (Blackburn, Taylor and Davis, 2010, p. 118).

Interviewed stakeholders highlighted that pressure by international bodies and foreign states have resulted in an increased focus on combatting trafficking in persons. As highlighted by the Ministry of Social Development and Human Security, the way to change the situation of trafficking in persons in Thailand has to start with the political will of the government. In this regard, the Ministry notes that the Prime Minister's focus on the issue has had an important impact. In 2015, Prime Minister Prayut raised the issue of human trafficking as a priority on the national agenda. Prime Minister Prayut also called for increased collaboration between the concerned agencies – which were previously reported to have worked in isolation from each other – and increased public officials' knowledge of trafficking in persons (Ministry of Foreign Affairs of the

Kingdom of Thailand, 2015). Collaboration has not only been increased between agencies, but also between agencies and international organisations. As an example, the Office of the National Anti-Corruption Commission (NACC) of Thailand has recently entered into a co-operation agreement with the International Organization for Migration (IOM) Thailand, with the goal of increasing knowledge and awareness of the relationship between corruption and human smuggling as well as corruption and human trafficking (Office of the National Anti-Corruption Commission of Thailand, 2015).

In addition to prioritising the fight against trafficking in persons, Prime Minister Prayut has also made strong statements on his commitment to fighting corruption in the public sector (Prayut, 2015). However, several government officials highlighted that the problem of a culture of corruption remains and that this will be difficult to change in the short term.

As late as March 2014, Thailand submitted a report on its 2013 trafficking record to the US State Department that, according to *The Guardian*, did not include any Rohingya in its total number of trafficked persons. *The Guardian* also reported that the Thai Ministry of Foreign affairs explained this by stating that "We have not found that the Rohingya are victims of human trafficking," and that "In essence, the Rohingya question is an issue of human smuggling" (Marshall and Sawitta Lefevre, 2014). During the interviews conducted by the OECD in August 2015, consulted stakeholders noted a positive change in perception or knowledge on the topic of trafficking. Stakeholders said that the situation of the Rohingya was previously perceived as a movement of migrants or a labour issue and not a trafficking problem. The lack of understanding that the Rohingya were being abused meant that actors such as the Royal Thai Police would use the "Immigration Act" when dealing with the issue, instead of the "Trafficking in Persons Act". The same applied for the situation on fishing boats. This was perceived as a conflict between employer and employee, and not an issue of human trafficking. In sum, stakeholders highlighted that officials in Thailand lacked knowledge and a general understanding of the problem of human trafficking, but that this is starting to change (Box 5.1).

Box 5.1. **Noteworthy case: The Rohingya**

As highlighted above, the Rohingya have generally not been classified as victims of trafficking. Examples of the government's stance include the aforementioned statements by the Thai Ministry of Foreign Affairs in March 2014 that "We have not found that the Rohingya are victims of human trafficking," and that "In essence, the Rohingya question is an issue of human smuggling" (Marshall and Sawitta Lefevre, 2014).However, there have been several reports over the years of the abuse the Rohingya have suffered in jungle camps. Human Rights Watch has reported that victims have starved to death or died of disease while held by traffickers (Human Rights Watch, 2015). A Reuters investigation into the case also found involvement of police in the trafficking of Rohingya. In 2014, Reuters reported on Thai immigration officials' practices of removing Rohingya refugees from Thailand's immigration detention centres and delivering them to human traffickers waiting at sea (Szep and Marshall, 2013). After this was done, the smuggling networks and human traffickers often took them back to Thailand's border camps, or to Malaysia (Marshall, 2014).

Box 5.1. **Noteworthy case: The Rohingya** *(continued)*

An even more recent case of Rohingya abuse and the involvement of public officials is from May 2015, when 36 bodies were found in an abandoned jungle prison camp near the Thai-Malaysian border (Holmes, 2015; *The Guardian*, 2015). The jungle camps were run by traffickers who held Rohingya migrants captive while extorting ransoms from their families before smuggling them into Malaysia (*Los Angeles Times*, 2015). Following the discovery, more than 50 people were arrested within a month. These included local politicians, government officials, police, and a senior-ranking army officer who was previously tasked with overseeing human trafficking issues in southern Thailand (*The Guardian*, 2015). Furthermore, about 50 police officers in charge of anti-trafficking, immigration, marine surveillance and border units in the southern provinces where the camps were found were removed from their posts pending investigations into their possible involvement in the human trafficking syndicates (*Los Angeles Times*, 2015; *The Guardian*, 2015). Some 15 state officials were also reported to be facing charges of negligence of their duty (*The Guardian*, 2015). In August 2015, the Royal Thai Police reported that 119 arrest warrants were out, that 73 persons had been arrested, and that 19 government officials were thought to be implicated.

In *Thailand's Trafficking in Persons 2014 Country Report*, the Thai Government reported that for 2014 and January 2015, there were "at least 5 cases in which over 236 Rohingya migrants or those who claimed to be Rohingya were rescued and 16 offenders are facing charges" (MSDHS, 2015, p. 9). The authorities also stated that "[a]ll cases that involved claims associated with Rohingya since 2014 have gone through a proper victim identification process, carried out by a multi-disciplinary team" (MSDHS, 2015, p. 9).

1. The Rohingya are a Muslim minority population that primarily lives in the Rakhine state in western Myanmar.

The Guiding Principles and Thailand

The following part of the chapter will highlight how the issues raised in the respective principles have been applied in the context of Thailand – and/or, if relevant, discuss any challenges or lessons learned in addressing the issue raised in the respective principles. Each sub-section will commence with a box stating the principle in question, followed by the application of it in Thailand.

1. International co-operation and agreements

Relevant international conventions are ratified and international co-operation against corruption and trafficking in persons is promoted.

In order to address the issue of trafficking in persons efficiently, there is a need to strengthen the legal basis against corruption and trafficking in persons. This could be done by strengthening international co-operation, and by countries joining international conventions and monitoring systems. It is important that national legislation on counter-trafficking is in line with international standards concerning trafficking in persons and corruption.

Thailand has ratified the United Nations "Convention Against Corruption" and is a signatory to the United Nations "Protocol to Prevent, Suppress and Punish Trafficking in Persons, Especially Women and Children, supplementing the United Nations Convention against Transnational Organized Crime" (United Nations, 2000). The aforementioned

Protocol – which is commonly referred to as the "Palermo Protocol" – has not yet been ratified by Thailand. Thailand has ratified several International Labour Organization (ILO) conventions, including the "Convention concerning Forced or Compulsory Labour (No. 29)", the "Convention concerning the Abolition of Forced Labour (No. 105)", and the "Convention concerning the Prohibition and Immediate Action for the Elimination of the Worst Forms of Child Labour (No. 182)". Thailand is also a signatory to the "ASEAN Declaration Against Trafficking in Persons Particularly Women and Children" (ASEAN, 2004).

In terms of bilateral co-operation, Thailand has signed a "Memorandum of Understanding (MOU) on Cooperation against Trafficking in Persons in the Greater Mekong Sub-Region" (2004) with four countries: Cambodia, the Lao PDR, Viet Nam, and Myanmar. MOUs are also being discussed with Malaysia, the United Arab Emirates, Brunei Darussalam, China, and India (MSDHS, 2015). In addition to bilateral agreements, there are also agreements between individual Thai government agencies and government agencies of neighbouring countries, and specific Thai government agencies and international organisations such as the ILO and IOM.

In terms of multilateral co-operation, Thailand is participating in the "Coordinated Mekong Ministerial Initiative against Trafficking" (COMMIT) and the "ASEANAPOL Framework", and takes part in the "Bali Process".[1]

Government agencies interviewed by the OECD highlighted that although these bilateral and multilateral agreements are useful, the joint action plans that are drafted after the agreements have been signed are what make the real difference. One of the problems highlighted in relation to bilateral MOUs is that it is sometimes difficult to get both sides to co-operate and be equally committed to the agreement. In terms of areas of improvement, one stakeholder highlighted that more work is needed in terms of co-operation with countries of origin. This co-operation should not only centre on trafficking in persons, but also on issues of corruption and how to combat this.

Processes of international co-operation in terms of mutual legal assistance and extradition are in place and functioning.

Trafficking in persons is often transnational in nature, with 66% of detected victims being trafficked across borders. However, the criminal justice responses to trafficking in persons generally only operate within national borders. Therefore, to efficiently be able to respond to trafficking in persons, countries would benefit from effective processes of international co-operation in terms of mutual legal assistance and extradition. An example of an initiative aimed at achieving this is the "Handbook on International Cooperation in Trafficking in Persons Cases"(ASEAN, 2010) for the ASEAN region. In order to be efficient, mutual legal assistance must allow for international identification, sequestration and seizure of assets accrued by traffickers, and the procedure of mutual legal assistance should be simplified, prioritised, and accelerated. Examples of how to improve cross-border co-operation could be to link regional trafficking in persons-focal points with regional anti-corruption focal points, and to identify and propose countermeasures to at-risk points of regional or transnational trafficking-in-persons-related corruption (for example the issuance of travel documents, border transfers and work permits). Law enforcement agencies should be encouraged to proactively share intelligence on transnational TIP networks. Law enforcement co-operation on intelligence is often an essential prerequisite to effective investigations, and it plays a complementary role to mutual legal assistance and subsequent prosecutions.

In terms of international co-operation on mutual legal assistance and extradition, Thailand has signed agreements on extradition with, for example, Myanmar (MSDHS, 2015), and is a signatory to the "ASEAN Mutual Legal Assistance Treaty". However, in the interviews and documentation reviewed, there is no information available on the number of extraditions that have taken place, or any information on potential work conducted to ensure that mutual legal processes are simplified, prioritised, and accelerated. The Thai government's *Thailand's Trafficking in Persons 2014 Country Report* only states that "[r]elevant agencies also utilise existing extradition agreements and Mutual Legal Assistance agreements with partner countries to prosecute traffickers" (MSDHS, 2015, p. 136). Data on extradition could be an area to prioritise moving forward.

There are several examples of cross-border co-operation between law enforcement agencies. To mention a few, police officers have been appointed as police attachés to the Royal Thai Embassies in Myanmar, Cambodia, and Yunnan, China, and 11 Border Liaison Offices have been established with the goal of facilitating co-ordination between border checkpoints of Thailand and Cambodia, Lao PDR, and Myanmar, respectively (MSDHS, 2015).

2. *Jointly addressing and investigating trafficking in persons and corruption with particular focus on at-risk sectors*

Strategies that address trafficking in persons and corruption, or include corruption issues in anti-trafficking plans, and vice versa, are in place.

Organised trafficking requires systemic corruption. However, few laws or strategies in place jointly address trafficking in persons and corruption. Due to the strong link between corruption/perceived levels of corruption with trafficking in persons, countries are therefore recommended to put in place strategies that jointly address corruption and trafficking in persons, or alternatively include corruption issues in anti-trafficking plans, and vice versa. By streamlining approaches, countries can address the issue by modifying anti-corruption tools or by simply including corruption issues in existing anti-trafficking measures, in particular in trainings and strategies. The importance of ensuring sufficient levels of political will to combat trafficking-in-persons-related corruption at all levels of government should not be underestimated, and the implementation of the laws in place needs to be prioritised.

As highlighted in the section on the legal framework, Thailand's "Anti-Trafficking in Persons Act B.E. 2551" does not specifically mention corruption or the link between corruption and trafficking. However, there are numerous paragraphs that could be used to address potential offences committed by public officials in the trafficking-in-persons process. These include those listed in Section 7 Paragraph 3 (assisting by any means so that the offender of trafficking in persons may not be arrested) and Paragraph 4 (demanding, accepting, or agreeing to accept a property or any other benefit in order to help the offender of trafficking in persons not to be punished). Furthermore, Section 13 lists the categories of public officials that are liable to twice the punishment for committing an offence under the Act. These include members of the House of Representatives, members of the Senate, members of a Local Administration Council, local administrators, government officials, employees of the Local Administration Organisation, or employees of an organisation or a public agency, members of a board, executives, or employees of state enterprise, officials, or members of a board of any organisation under the Constitution. If the person is a member of the Committee, member of Sub-Committee, or a member of any working group and competent official empowered to act in accordance with the "Anti-Trafficking in Persons Act", the punishment for committing an offence is three times the punishment stipulated for such an offence.

Although there are numerous examples of how the government has communicated a zero-tolerance of corruption, there are few examples on where the link between corruption and TIP is addressed, or where specific interventions proposed promote the issues of understanding and combatting corruption in the TIP chain. One such example is Announcement No. 68/2557 on "Urgent Interim Measures to Prevent and Suppress Human Trafficking and Solve Problems pertaining to Migrant Workers, Phase One", by the National Council for Peace and Order that was issued on 17 June 2014. It stipulates that "if any government officer fails to carry out the duty or is involved in illegal exploitation of human trafficking, in particular concerning migrant workers, child labour, women, and migrant labour smuggling, such officer shall be punished through both disciplinary and criminal proceedings" (Ministry of Foreign Affairs of the Kingdom of Thailand, 2014).

The government has also set up what they term as two major groups of hotlines: Human Trafficking-related Hotlines and Anti-Corruption Hotlines (MSDHS, 2015). Reports of incidences related to corruption or government officials' complicity in human trafficking can be made to agencies such as the Office of Public Sector Anti-Corruption and the Anti-Money Laundering Office, and reports of incidences of human trafficking can be reported to the Ministry of Human Development and Human Security, the Anti-Human Trafficking Division of the Royal Thai Police, the Damrongdhama Centre (the Ministry of Interior) and the Department of Special Investigation (MSDHS, 2015). Although these initiatives are welcomed, this division of the reporting can be seen as an indication of a continued compartmentalisation of the two issues, instead of a joint approach to addressing TIP-related corruption. A suggestion would therefore be to introduce one hotline where those reporting on trafficking in persons can also submit reports on corruption related to the incident they are calling about.

Sectors prone to trafficking-in-persons-related corruption are given priority in the implementation of relevant strategies.

When implementing the relevant strategies that address trafficking-in-persons-related corruption, countries are advised to identify and pay particular attention to vulnerable sectors and industries in their specific country context and steps that could be taken to prevent or combat the exploitation of people. This could, for example, entail regulation of labour-intensive sectors, in particular the construction, brothel, agriculture, fishing and textile industries or the foreign labour recruitment sector in a country. Countries are recommended to involve non-governmental actors as well as the private sector in the identification of at-risk sectors and the monitoring of these.

Thailand is one of the world's largest exporters of seafood (FAO, 2012). In an ILO study published in 2013, 17% of around 600 surveyed fishermen in Thailand said that they worked against their will, and 15% stated that they were unable to leave for threat of financial penalties, violence, or the threat of violence (ILO, 2013). In a 2009 study conducted by the UN Inter-Agency Project on Human Trafficking, 59% of victims reported witnessing a murder by the boat captain (UNIAP, 2009).

In order to address the issues in the fishery sector, Thailand has recently enacted a number of new laws. These include the "Fishery Act B.E. 2558" (2015), the Ministry of Labour's "Regulation to Protect Labour in the Sea Fishing Industry B.E. 2557" (2014), and the Marine Department's "Regulation on Criteria for Permission to Work in Fishing Vessels of 30 Gross Tonnage Capacity or Over B.E. 2557" (2014). The Ministry of Labour's "Regulation to Protect Labour in the Sea Fishing Industry B.E. 2557" stipulates a minimum age of 18 years for workers on sea vessels; a minimum rest period of at least ten hours; a labour contract signed with the consent of both parties; and 30 days minimum annual leave (Seafish, 2015; MSDHS, 2015). Furthermore, the Thai government requires fishing vessel owners to submit lists of their crews and register them at One Stop Service Centres in 22 coastal provinces (MSDHS, 2015). Joint inspections are carried out by the Department of Fisheries, the Marine Department, the Marine Police Division and the Royal Thai Navy, Department of Labour Protection and Welfare, and the Department of Employment. Some 456 inspections were reported to have been carried out between October 2014 and September 2015 (Prompoj, 2015). This joint approach and co-operation between agencies – with a particular focus on the successful initiatives of information sharing between involved actors – was highlighted as a best practice by several stakeholders interviewed by the OECD. There was a call for similar initiatives to be implemented when addressing other crimes.

In relation to the drafting or implementation processes of these laws, the stakeholders working on corruption stated that they were not consulted. There is therefore room for further improvement in terms of consultations in the drafting process of laws governing the fishery sector in order to address the issues of corruption and public officials' involvement in trafficking.

Information and resources are leveraged and shared among relevant actors.

Cases of trafficking and corruption are often dealt with separately. According to the United Nations Office on Drugs and Crime (UNODC), there is a lack of referral to the relevant authorities of: 1) cases of trafficking in persons where there are indicators for corruption; and 2) referral of corruption cases where there are indicators of trafficking in persons. Co-operation is therefore essential among relevant actors to share information and resources. This can be done through the establishment of taskforces or joint operations. It is also crucial to establish protocols between non-governmental organisations (NGOs) and law enforcement bodies to co-ordinate their activities so that both sides understand and acknowledge the efforts and responsibilities of the other.

Furthermore, anti-money laundering systems can be used to detect and prevent the financing of trafficking in persons, and assist in the confiscation of profits from trafficking in persons as well as the prevention of the reinvestment of illicit funds into the criminal trafficking networks. Financial intelligence systems that are already in place can be used to map the activities of trafficking networks and how these networks interact with corrupt officials.

Stakeholders interviewed by the OECD reported that it is easy to reach out to other departments or agencies in order to ask for input or information and to share experiences. However, no concrete examples of joint operations that specifically address TIP-related corruption were identified. The co-operation mechanisms or centres that have been set up appeared to mostly bring together actors working on trafficking in persons, without including actors with a specific expertise on corruption.

According to the 2015 US *Trafficking in Persons Report*, the Anti-Money Laundering Office (AMLO) reported that 107 money laundering cases associated with suspected human trafficking are under investigation. Two noteworthy examples are: 1) a case in relation to human trafficking in the form of prostitution in the Narathiwat Province where the AMLO seized THB 2 million; and 2) a case from the Songkhla Province which involved 53 female victims where the AMLO seized THB 30 million (USD 1 million) (MSDHS, 2015). Considering the size of this illicit trade, there is however room for further improvement in terms of seizure of assets accrued by traffickers.

Corruption is also investigated when investigating trafficking in persons.

According to the Council of Europe, investigations and prosecutions of trafficking in persons should be accompanied by investigations into corruption and finances of suspects. In order to effectively deal with trafficking-in-persons-related corruption, indicators need to be developed for actors working in the field of trafficking in persons to detect corruption when investigating trafficking cases.

The Ministry of Social Development and Human Security is the Thai agency responsible for conducting interviews with trafficking victims. They reported that they do not have any specific interview questions that ask about potential involvement by government officials in the trafficking process. However, representatives from the Ministry of Social Development and Human Security stated that if any information about a public official's involvement comes up during the interview, this is reported to the relevant agencies. According to Dr. Leslie Holmes, "even researchers have been either slow or reluctant to consider including questions about possible collusion between corrupt officials and traffickers when surveying trafficked persons" (Holmes, 2009, p. 84). This is an area where improvements could be made.

In 2014, the Thai government reported that a total of 19 public officials faced criminal charges or disciplinary punishments for their involvement in trafficking (MSDHS, 2015). As an example of criminal charges, the Public Sector Anti-Corruption Commission (PACC) launched an investigation against three police officers from the Highway Police, the Immigration Bureau, and the Special Unit of the Pattani Provincial Police in the Pattani Province. They were charged on accounts of human trafficking, restriction of freedom and extortion, and abuse of power to detain three Cambodian nationals for exploitative purposes (MSDHS, 2015). As an example of disciplinary punishments, 11 police officers were removed from their previous posts for negligence and dereliction of duty, and were transferred to inactive posts (MSDHS, 2015).

Specialised multi-agency units are established and multi-agency trainings are organised.

At the national level, countries could enhance co-operation between anti-corruption and anti-trafficking practitioners, for example through multi-agency training and specialised multi-agency units staffed by prosecutors and selected police.

Although there are several examples of multi-agency teams – such as, for example, the victim identification teams composed of officials from the Ministry of Social Development and Human Security and the Ministry of Interior (MSDHS, 2015) – and multi-agency trainings being organised on the topic of trafficking in persons, there have not been any reports from interviewed stakeholders on any involvement of anti-corruption stakeholders in these initiatives. This is a suggestion for improvement moving forward.

3. Transparency and an integrity framework for public officials at risk

Specific rules/standards of behaviour – such as guidelines or codes of conduct – with respect to corruption and trafficking for public officials at risk are in place. The violations of the codes of conduct entail sanctions.

The conduct of the international peacekeepers, civilian police, intergovernmental and non-governmental organisations' staff and diplomatic personnel has raised serious concerns in relation to trafficking in persons and corruption. According to the cases analysed by the Council of Europe, the problem is reported to be particularly widespread among the police. One way of addressing this can be to include specific rules/standards of behaviour with respect to corruption and trafficking, for example in codes of conduct. As supervision, discipline, and accountability are key in preventing and combating corruption, effective mechanisms are needed for reporting, investigating and sanctioning the violation of these codes of conduct for officials at risk.

Many of the sectors of public officials that could play a role in trafficking in persons are already covered by codes of conduct. However, some of these codes may need to be updated in order to address the specific issues relating to trafficking in persons. UNODC has proposed a number of specific measures that countries can implement, for example requesting police staff who are conducting brothel raids to always be accompanied by one or more colleagues, preferably female staff, when conducting raids in brothels.

In 2014, 19 public officials faced criminal charges or disciplinary sanctions in relation to human trafficking, negligence, or involvement in the second degree (MSDHS, 2015). Officials who are facing charges are removed from their posts until the cases against them have been tried (MSDHS, 2015).

Chapter 6, Section 85, of the "Civil Service Act B.E. 2551" (Kingdom of Thailand, 2008b) lists a number of disciplinary breaches that could be relevant in the case of public officials' involvement in human trafficking, such as wrongfully performing or refraining to perform official duties, committing an act which is attributable as a gross misconduct, or committing a criminal offence. Section 88 of the same chapter stipulates five types of disciplinary sanctions: written reprimand; deduction of salary; reduction of salary; dismissal; and expulsion. Within each Ministry, there is a Ministerial Civil Service Commission that, among other duties, is in charge of matters pertaining to disciplinary proceedings and orders of discharge from government service.

As previously highlighted, public officials' involvement is also regulated through the "Anti-Trafficking in Persons Act B.E. 2551", where public officials – depending on their position – face two to three times the punishment stipulated for the offences established by the Act.

Except for the legal requirements listed above, the interviews conducted with stakeholders in Thailand did not highlight any specific initiatives in relation to rules or standards of conduct or specific measures that address the link between human trafficking and corruption.

The activities of staff working in sectors at risk are performed in a transparent manner.

Sectors at specific risk of corruption in the trafficking-in-persons context need to ensure that their staff's activities are performed in a transparent manner and that unnecessary bureaucracy is eliminated so that the opportunities for corrupt officials to seek bribes are limited. This is particularly relevant within law enforcement (e.g. border control, customs and immigration authorities) and criminal justice authorities. As raised by UNODC, ensuring that the staff's activities are performed in a transparent manner does not necessarily mean public disclosure of assets and private interests but rather safeguards, such as, for example, internal approval systems of tasks to be performed and avoiding having one-to-one meetings with individuals such as visa and work permit applicants, presumed trafficking victims, and suspects. In addition, independent legal audit of trafficking cases could be conducted in order to assure that cases were handled in a correct manner.

During the interviews conducted in Bangkok with representatives from different government agencies, no specific initiatives with the goal of increasing the transparency of public officials' activities were highlighted.

An additional audit component has been introduced at the Royal Thai Police. All cases from 2014 will be reviewed by a general with the Royal Thai Police in order to ensure that the investigations were conducted in a correct manner. However, it could be questioned if this is in line with the Guiding Principle's second part – ensuring that unnecessary bureaucracy is eliminated.

A wider framework of integrity for public officials is promoted.

In addition to establishing rules/standards on behaviour of public officials in respect to corruption and trafficking, countries can benefit from promoting a wider framework ensuring the integrity of public officials, including: asset disclosure regime; conflict of interest legislation; and whistleblower protection. Of particular focus are issues such as outside positions for police officers (for example when police officers take up positions as security guards for bars and clubs). Officials at risk should also receive general anti-corruption training which could contribute to the prevention and combating of corruption in trafficking in persons. These need to be context specific and address potential issues such as cultures of corruption and gift-giving.

According to Chapter 3 of the "Organic Act on Counter Corruption B.E. 2542" (Kingdom of Thailand, 1999) that was amended in "B.E. 2550" (2007) and "B.E. 2554" (2011), a person holding a political position (Prime Minister, Minister, Member of the House of Representatives, Senator, political officials, political parliamentary officials, local administrators, deputy local administrator, assistant local administrator, and member of a local assembly of a local government organisation) have to submit statements of their assets and liabilities upon taking office and vacating the office. A number of other officials (President of the Supreme Court of Justice, President of the Constitutional Court, President of the Supreme Administrative Court, Prosecutor General, Election Commissioner, Ombudsman, Judge of the Constitutional Court, member of the State Audit Commission, Vice President of the Supreme Court of Justice, Vice President of the Supreme Administrative Court, Chief of the Military Judicial Office, judge of the Supreme Court of Justice, judge of the Supreme Administrative Court, Deputy Prosecutor General, or persons holding high ranking positions) have to submit declarations every three years while holding that office, as well as upon vacation of the office in question (Section 39). However, the Act does not stipulate any disclosure requirements for lower ranking officials – such as, for example, police officers.

The "Organic Act on Counter Corruption" also regulates conflicts of interest for state officials, which covers a much wider range of officials than the disclosure requirements above. Section 100 of the Act states that state officials should not have an interest in a contract made with a government agency; be a partner or shareholder in a partnership or company that is a party to a contract made with a government agency; be a concessionaire or continue to hold a concession from the State, State agency, State enterprise or local administration; be a party to a contract monopolistic nature made with the State, a government agency, State agency, State enterprise or local administration; or have an interest in the capacity of director, counsel, representative, official or employee in a private business which is under supervision, control or audit of the State agency that the State official is attached to or where the State official performs duties in the capacity as State official. The last point applies provided that the nature of the interest of the private business is contrary to or inconsistent with the public interest or the interest of the government service, or that it may affect the State official's independence in performing his duties. This could be applicable in the example of police officers taking up positions as security guards for bars and clubs that is listed in the Guiding Principles.

In September 1999, the Office of the Civil Service Commission established the Ethics Promotion and Information Center. The Center has four main functions:

1. Research and development, where the tasks include the formulation of ethical standards, the development of ethics promotion strategies, and to serve as a contact point for the exchange of knowledge and experience in the field of ethics promotion with domestic and international networks.
2. Co-ordinating ethical promotion, where the tasks include the provision of policy and implementation guidance to government agencies on the topic of ethics promotion in public service. Ethics Promotion Committees are created at the ministerial, departmental, and provincial levels to build networks promoting a clean and transparent civil service.
3. Public relations, where activities include the development of ethics promotion campaigns in various media.
4. Trainings.

In relation to trainings, the Center develops ethics courses and training materials, and provides training-the-trainers workshops. The ethics courses' target groups range from the newly recruited to experienced officials and team leaders. The trainings are based on the policies and laws in place that relate to the promotion of good governance, including Section 279 of the Constitution (B.E. 2550) (Kingdom of Thailand, 2007) on the "Ethics of Holders of Political Positions and State Officials", Section 78 of the "Civil Service Act (B.E. 2551)" on "Upholding the Ethics of Officials", the "Civil Service Code (B.E. 2010)", and government policies on the topic.

In addition to conducting trainings, the Office of the Civil Service Commission also promotes ethics by arranging an annual ceremony where public officials pledge an oath of allegiance to His Majesty the King that includes committing themselves to serving the country with honesty and integrity. Another ethics promotion tool employed by the Office of the Civil Service Commission is the Civil Servant of the Year Award that is presented to winners by the Prime Minister on the April 1st Civil Service Day. This award was highlighted as one of the success stories in promoting ethics and awarding outstanding civil servants in Thailand.

Mechanisms that allow for public officials as well as the public to expose misconduct and report dishonest or illegal activity and that ensure the effective protection from retaliation are in place.

Confidential hotlines or similar measures for whistleblowers may be established so that public officials or private sector employees that witness corrupt behaviour by their colleagues can provide information about these activities. This can be established within government organisations as well as international organisations. Members of the public may also be given clear channels for exposing misconduct and reporting dishonest or illegal activity occurring in public and private sector organisations. Countries need to ensure that whistleblowers are effectively protected from retaliation and intimidation.

The Prime Minister has established a Centre to Combat Corruption within the Office of Public Sector Anti-Corruption Commission that is responsible for receiving complaints from the public about corruption and misconduct by public officials. In addition, there are several anti-corruption hotlines where citizens can report misconduct or dishonest or illegal activity. These include 1205 by the National Anti-Corruption Commission, 1206 by the Office of the Public Sector Anti-Corruption Commission, 1710 by the Anti-Money Laundering Office, and 1300 by the Ministry of Social Development and Human Security.

According to the National Anti-Corruption Commission, they have the right to start an investigation from any type of source. This could range from anything from letters sent to the NACC, to journalists' reports published in newspapers.

The government has recently approved amendments to the "Anti-Trafficking in Persons Act B.E. 2551" from 2008. Among the passed amendments is the protection of whistleblowers (US Department of State, 2015).

The recruitment process of officials is transparent, competitive and subject to independent scrutiny. Upon recruitment, officials receive training, adequate supervision and are subject to regular performance evaluations.

Recruitment of key officials, in particular those employed in anti-corruption or anti-trafficking units, prosecutors and judicial officials needs to be consistently conducted by means of a transparent and competitive selection process that is subject to independent scrutiny. Upon recruitment, key officials would benefit from receiving training, adequate supervision and be subject to regular performance evaluations. It is important that the training does not only cover instructions relating to specific tasks and responsibilities that the employee will encounter, but also the standards of conduct and values of the organisation.

In general, people who want to enter the public service have to pass a competitive examination that is issued by the Office of the Civil Service Commission (OCSC). However, there are a number of exceptions to this rule that are listed in Sections 55, 56, 63, 64 and 65 of the "Civil Service Act, B.E. 2551" (2008). As an example, Section 56 states that "A ministry or department which has exceptional reasons and necessities may instate persons possessing high levels of knowledge, competence and expertise to the government service and appoint to knowledge worker positions at professional, senior professional, expert or advisory levels, or to general positions at highly skilled level, pursuant to rules, procedures and conditions prescribed by the CSC." Rules and guidelines on the process, conditions and criteria for selection under the exceptions are stipulated in Civil Service Commission Circulars that are available on the Office of the Civil Service Commission's website. Such circulars require departments to publicly announce information about the vacant positions, job specifications, the application process, the selection methods, the selection criteria, and lists of candidates who passed the selection. Cases that do not conform with the guidelines are required to be submitted to the Civil Service Commission for consideration. The transparency of these types of procedures is important to ensure that the general public as well as other non-successful candidates are able to scrutinise the appointments made.

During the interviews conducted for this report, the Office of the Civil Service Commission highlighted a new initiative that they are working on that focuses on giving more weight to ethics in the hiring of high-ranking officials in the civil service. The goal would be to include ethics as a criterion in their selection process. While encouraging, a key challenge that needs to be addressed in order to implement this initiative is how to measure the ethics of a candidate.

Key officials receive training so that they are able to correctly identify trafficking victims, understand the nature of the crime, and recognise warning signs throughout the different stages of the trafficking-in-persons process.

In order to correctly identify and deal with trafficking-in-persons cases, it is essential that key officials receive training. Experience shows that the first government official a victim of trafficking is likely to meet is a local police officer and not a lawmaker or diplomat, and if this local police officer has not been trained to identify trafficking victims and understand the crime, there is a heightened risk that the crime is not properly identified. Also, for example consular staff in countries of origin may benefit from exchanging experiences and being trained in recognising visa applications that could involve trafficking in persons.

In 2014, the Thai government reported that 445 participants from the Royal Thai Police, the Royal Thai Navy, the Department of Special Investigation (DSI), the Department of Labour Protection and Welfare, the Department of Employment, the Ministry of Public Health, and the Ministry of Social Development and Human Security received training on the "Anti-Trafficking in Persons Act" (MSDHS, 2015). Also, 100 participants from the Ministry of Social Development and Human Security received training on victim identification (MSDHS, 2015). Although these trainings are important in raising awareness and knowledge on TIP, they will need to be scaled up to reach much larger audiences. To put the numbers in perspective, the Royal Thai Police Force is currently estimated to employ around 230 000 officers (Interpol, 2015). In conducting the trainings, it is important to ensure that they also reach local law enforcement officers, since these are most likely the first government official a trafficking victim meets.

Another initiative to improve the victim identification process includes a newly designed screening questionnaire to be used by police officers to ensure more accurate identification of victims (MSDHS, 2015).

4. Awareness-raising and prevention measures for public officials and the general public

Public awareness regarding the existence, causes, and gravity of trafficking in persons and the active participation of individuals and groups outside the public sector in the prevention of, and the fight against, trafficking-in-persons-related corruption is promoted.

The importance of prevention measures is not consistently recognised. Article 13 of the United Nations Convention against Corruption (UNCAC) (United Nations, 2003) UNCAC demands that each State Party shall take the appropriate measures to promote the "active participation of individuals and groups outside the public sector, such as civil society, non-governmental organisations and community-based organisations, in the prevention of and the fight against corruption and to raise public awareness regarding the existence, causes and gravity of and the threat posed by corruption." Specific measures to strengthen this participation include:

1. enhancing the transparency of, and promoting the contribution of, the public to decision-making processes
2. ensuring that the public has effective access to information
3. undertaking public information activities that contribute to non-tolerance of corruption, as well as public education programmes, including school and university curricula
4. respecting, promoting and protecting the freedom to seek, receive, publish and disseminate information concerning corruption.

Similarly, Article 9(2) of the United Nations "Protocol to Prevent, Suppress and Punish Trafficking in Persons, Especially Women and Children", establishes that State Parties shall "endeavour to undertake such measures such as research, information and mass media campaigns and social and economic initiatives to prevent and combat trafficking in persons." The Council of Europe suggests giving particular attention to the development of special awareness programmes in schools.

In order to effectively raise awareness of the linkages between corruption and trafficking in persons, countries can involve and train media and facilitate investigative journalism on trafficking in persons and corruption. Furthermore, media can play an important role in increasing public awareness and knowledge on TIP and corruption hotspots, deterring offenders by highlighting arrests and prosecutions, and rewarding and encouraging successful law enforcement through the publication of success stories.

The Thai government carried out a number of awareness-raising initiatives and campaigns in 2014. Examples include the organisation of the annual Anti-Trafficking in Persons Day campaign in Bangkok and in ten other provinces to raise awareness about trafficking. The campaign included activities such as broadcasting information through different media outlets and presenting awards to those who have made significant contributions towards the fight against human trafficking (MSDHS, 2015). Other examples include the production of 106 billboards/information posters and 1 183 workshops conducted on the dangers and negative impact of human trafficking (MSDHS, 2015). In 2014, "mobile units" were also launched with the goal of enhancing public awareness on child labour and human trafficking. The Thai government reports that the units attracted and educated 196 669 employers, employees, parents and members of the communities throughout 2014 (MSDHS, 2015). Although these activities all indicate an increased focus on awareness raising by the Thai government, these initiatives – as highlighted by the US Department of State's 2015 *Trafficking in Persons Report* – continued to concentrate on Thai populations and did not adequately reach out to migrant populations. More trainings for migrant workers from Myanmar, Lao PDR, and Cambodia – such as those that will be discussed in a section below – will be needed (MSDHS, 2015).

In terms of involving the media, the Ministry of Social Development and Human Security discussed a project that will shortly be carried out in communities along the Thai border. The purpose of the project is to train media on the concept of human trafficking and inform them of where citizens can submit reports so that reporters in turn can relay this information to the local communities through their radio programmes. The idea is that by increased education through radio, the local communities can help keep their communities safe and report on suspicious activities. If this pilot is successful, it could be replicated in other provinces as well as other countries.

While there are examples of where the media is encouraged to participate and report on trafficking crimes, there are also cases where government interventions have acted as deterrents. The US Department of State's 2015 *Trafficking in Persons Report* notes that "the Thai Navy's 2013 defamation lawsuit against two journalists for reporting on trafficking crimes remained pending. The Prime Minister's public comments in late March 2015 discouraged reporting on trafficking in the fishing sector. Fear of defamation suits or retaliation also likely discouraged journalists from reporting and law enforcement officials from pursuing trafficking cases" (US Department of State, 2015, p. 332). Further work to promote reporting and scrutiny by journalists is needed.

Targeted awareness-raising measures for all parties involved in anti-trafficking issues are provided.

In addition to general anti-corruption measures, specific awareness-raising measures that highlight vulnerabilities, responsibilities, risks, and draw attention to how corrupt behaviour could facilitate the crime of trafficking in persons and the re-victimisation of the trafficked victims are essential to understand the links and forms of trafficking. Consequently, these measures need to be provided for all parties involved in anti-trafficking issues, including police and anti-trafficking organisations.

In the OECD interviews conducted with government agencies, there were no reports of specific awareness-raising measures that focused on how corrupt behaviour could facilitate the crime of trafficking. Moving forward, there is a need for the issues of corruption and human trafficking to be better integrated in the different initiatives being implemented by the Thai government. Under the current model, the two issues are largely treated separately from each other, without any focus on how the two are linked.

Preventive measures for potential victims of trafficking in persons are in place, in particular offering counselling about corruption and trafficking before and after they have undertaken a migration journey and alerting communities of early signs of corruption.

It is essential to build civic response and community awareness about the linkages between corruption and trafficking in persons. Specific measures proposed by the UNODC for potential victims of trafficking include: 1) alerting communities that early signs of corruption in a legitimate migration journey should be considered as warning indicators that trafficking may be taking place; and 2) giving citizens access to free, confidential counselling about corruption and trafficking before and after they have undertaken a migration journey, in order to make them aware of their rights and capable of looking for help if they are infringed in a way that renders them victims of trafficking.

For 2014, the Thai government reported on a number of initiatives to prevent trafficking in persons. One example includes 13 trainings on preventive measures that were organised for 850 police officers and 8 566 members of the public. The trainings aimed at creating a better understanding of the various approaches used in combating human trafficking, and how participants could avoid becoming victims of trafficking (MSDHS, 2015). Another example is the preparatory trainings that were provided to 52 000 Thai workers before they departed on their work overseas. The trainings focused on general information on the countries they were going to, information on how to report any problems to the Thai authorities, and how to protect themselves against exploitation (MSDHS, 2015). Trainings were also provided for 14 864 migrant workers from Myanmar, Lao PDR, and Cambodia. These trainings focused on their rights and responsibilities, the rules and regulations that apply to them, as well as traditions and culture (MSDHS, 2015).

Another preventive measure that was taken in 2014 was to sign Memorandums of Understanding with Lao PDR, Myanmar, and Cambodia with the goal of employing more migrant workers through government-to-government arrangements. Work permit fees were also reduced from THB 2 000 to THB 500 with the goal of creating greater incentive for migrant workers to use formal channels in taking up work in Thailand. This in turn would reduce their vulnerability to debt bondage, forced labour, and human trafficking (MSDHS, 2015). In 2014, 10 164 Thai workers secured their jobs overseas through this sort of government-supported arrangement (MSDHS, 2015).

5. *Improvement of data collection and systematic use of information*

Data on trafficking in persons are collected, analysed and used systematically.

Most countries are not systematically collecting and analysing data on investigations or prosecutions of public officials relating to trafficking in persons and corruption. There are many reasons for the scarcity of data. Among the most important reasons highlighted by the International Organization for Migration (IOM) are the victims' reluctance to report or testify for fear of reprisals; lack of harmonisation among existing data sources; and the opposition of some countries and agencies to share data. As a crucial step in addressing trafficking-in-persons-related corruption, countries need to focus on the collection of data and information in order to get a better insight into the problem. Because of its transnational nature, data on trafficking-in-persons-related corruption also needs to be collected and aggregated at the regional level. It should be stressed that any legal provisions or policy decisions on data collection and/or the creation of databases need to be accompanied by a commitment of resources for implementation.

Information on corruption provided by victims and NGOs can also be used more systematically. Government agencies working on anti-corruption and anti-trafficking need to co-operate with the non-governmental sector and civil society to ensure that information and experiences from victims are collected (through, for example, interviews) and that this information is passed on to the anti-corruption and anti-trafficking units in government. By improving the data collection and systemic use of information, countries would be allowed to implement targeted responses based on facts.

Although the Office of the Civil Service Commission collects data on breaches and disciplinary sanctions in relation to misconduct by public officials, the data is not made publicly available and the statistics of cases are not published on line. Data is made available upon request to other departments or ministries, but it is not provided proactively in a joint database.

There is a human trafficking database that has been set up together with the Ministry of Social Development and Human Security (MSDHS). The Royal Thai Police enters data on investigated cases and legal proceedings against offenders, and the MSDHS enters data on victims of human trafficking (MSDHS, 2015). The database is not publicly available. Furthermore, the database does not sort data or collect statistics on corruption in relation to trafficking in persons. The MSDHS stated that the cases highlighted in *Thailand's Trafficking in Persons 2014 Country Report* should be seen as examples, and not a complete account of all cases where public officials could have been involved in trafficking. Similarly to the example of the database, there is no tracking of the number of cases where corruption is mentioned in the calls received through the MSDHS's hotline.

Suggestions moving forward would be to make it possible to generate statistics on cases of corruption in the database and in the cases reported to the various hotlines in place. Furthermore, there is room for improvement in terms of including questions on corruption and the involvement of public officials in the victim interviews. For a more in-depth discussion on this, see the Guiding Principle on investigating corruption when investigating trafficking in persons.

6. Lift immunity in corruption and trafficking cases

Immunity from prosecution of public officials is duly lifted to allow for effective investigation, prosecution and adjudication of corruption and trafficking-in-persons-related offences.

The purpose of immunity is to protect the independence of public officials and make sure that they will make difficult decisions without risking facing personal consequences for this decision (e.g. being sued). According to UNCAC Article 30(2), "Each State Party shall take such measures as may be necessary to establish or maintain, in accordance with its legal system and constitutional principles, an appropriate balance between any immunities or jurisdictional privileges accorded to its public officials for the performance of their functions and the possibility, when necessary, of effectively investigating, prosecuting and adjudicating offences established in accordance with this Convention." Similarly, in cases of trafficking in persons, countries need to lift the immunity from prosecution of public officials following an allegation of corruption that is supported by evidence.

According to the National Anti-Corruption Commission of Thailand, public officials are not immune to prosecution.

Stakeholders' feedback on the Guiding Principles and findings from the in-country testing

The "Guiding Principles on Combatting Corruption related to Trafficking in Persons" were well received by both government agencies and non-governmental organisations. The testing of the Guiding Principles showed that they not only reflect many of the good practices that country representatives highlighted, but that they also raise recommendations in areas where more work is needed to effectively address trafficking-in-persons-related corruption.

During the in-country consultations, stakeholders highlighted the Guiding Principles' detailed nature and the inclusion of specific examples on how to implement the different recommendations as particularly useful. In the case of Thailand, several stakeholders highlighted the importance of political will from the highest levels of government in putting the issue of human trafficking on the agenda, and making it a priority within government agencies. The same also applied for the work against corruption in the private sector.

Stakeholders also stated that although they were of the opinion that international agreements were valuable, what was even more useful for their work was the specific action plans that they discuss and draft after the agreement has been signed. Without the creation of the joint action plans, the international agreements would – according to interviewed stakeholders – simply be agreements on paper that would not be implemented.

In relation to the promotion of integrity within the public sector, interviewed stakeholders highlighted the government's initiatives of positive reinforcement through awards given to outstanding civil servants as a best practice from Thailand.

Note

1. The "Bali Process on People Smuggling, Trafficking in Persons and Related Transnational Crime" is a voluntary forum that brings together over 45 members – composed of national governments and international agencies – with the purpose of raising regional awareness, and developing and implementing strategies and practical co-operation in response to people smuggling, trafficking in persons and related transnational crime. For more information, see www.baliprocess.net.

References

ASEAN (Association of Southeast Asian Nations) (2010), *ASEAN Handbook on International Legal Cooperation in Trafficking in Persons Cases*, ASEAN Secretariat, Jakarta, www.unodc.org/documents/human-trafficking/ASEAN Handbook on_ International_Legal_Cooperation_in_TIPCases.pdf.

ASEAN (2004), "ASEAN Declaration Against Trafficking in Persons Particularly Women and Children", Vientiane, 29 November, www1.umn.edu/ humanrts/research/Philippines/ASEAN%20Declaration%20Against%20Trafficking%20in%20Persons%20Particularly%20Women%20and%20Children.pdf.

Blackburn, A. G., R. W. Taylor and J. E. Davis (2010), "Understanding the complexities of human trafficking and child sexual exploitation: The case of Southeast Asia", *Women and Criminal Justice,* 20(1-2), pp. 105-126.

European Commission (2015), "EU acts on illegal fishing: Yellow card issued to Thailand while South Korea and Philippines are cleared", press release, http://europa.eu/rapid/press-release_IP-15-4806_en.htm.

FAO (Food and Agriculture Organization of the United Nations) (2012), *The State of World Fisheries and Aquaculture 2012*, FAO, Rome.

Governments of the Kingdom of Cambodia, the People's Republic of China, the Lao People's Democratic Republic, the Union of Myanmar, the Kingdom of Thailand and the Socialist Republic of Vietnam (2004), "Memorandum of Understanding on Cooperation against Trafficking in Persons in the Greater Mekong Sub-Region", Yangon, 29 October, www.no-trafficking.org/reports_docs/commit/commit_eng_ mou.pdf.

Holmes, O. (2015), "Thailand dismisses US criticism over human trafficking and slavery", *The Guardian*, 28 July, www.theguardian.com/world/2015/jul/28/thailand-us-human-trafficking-slavery-report.

Holmes, L. (2009), "Human Trafficking and Corruption: Triple Victimisation?", in C. Friesendorf (ed.), *Strategies Against Human Trafficking: The Role of the Security Sector*, : National Defence Academy and Austrian Ministry of Defence and Sports, Vienna and Geneva, pp. 83-114.

Human Rights Watch (2015), "Thailand: Mass Graves of Rohingya Found in Trafficking Camp", www.hrw.org/news/2015/05/01/thailand-mass-graves-rohingya-found-trafficking-camp.

ILO (International Labour Organization) (2013), *Employment Practices and Working Conditions in Thailand's Fishing Sector*, ILO/Asian Research Center for Migration, Institute of Asian Studies, Chulalongkorn University, Thailand.

ILO (1999), "Worst Forms of Child Labour Convention, 1999 (No. 182)", Geneva, 17 June, www.ilo.org/dyn/normlex/en/f?p=NORMLEXPUB:12100:0::NO:12100: P12100_ILO_CODE:C182.

ILO (1957), "Abolition of Forced Labour Convention, 1957 (No. 105)", ILO, Geneva, 25 June, www.ilo.org/dyn/normlex/en/f?p=1000:12100:0::NO::P12100_ILO_CODE:C105.

ILO (1930), "Forced Labour Convention, 1930 (No. 29)", Geneva, 28 June, www.ilo.org/dyn/normlex/en/f?p=NORMLEXPUB:12100:0::NO::P12100_INSTRUMENT_ID:312174.

Interpol (2015), "Thailand: Royal Thai Police", www.interpol.int/Member-countries/Asia-South-Pacific/Thailand.

Kingdom of Thailand (2015), "Fishery Act, B.E. 2558", www.fisheries.go.th/law/images%5Cdatanew%5Cpr7.doc.

Kingdom of Thailand (2014a), "Regulation to Protect Labour in the Sea Fishing Industry, B.E. 2557".

Kingdom of Thailand (2014b), Regulation on Criteria for Permission to Work in Fishing Vessels of 30 Gross Tonnage Capacity or Over, B.E. 2557".

Kingdom of Thailand (2008a), "The Anti-Trafficking in Persons Act, B.E. 2551", www.no-trafficking.org/content/Laws_Agreement/laws_agreement_pdf/trafficking_in_persons_act_b.e%202551%20(eng.).pdf.

Kingdom of Thailand (2008b), "Civil Service Act, B.E. 2551", www.ocsc.go.th/ocsc/en/files/Civil_Service_Act_B_E_2551.pdf.

Kingdom of Thailand (2007), "Constitution of the Kingdom of Thailand, B.E. 2550", www.unodc.org/tldb/pdf/Thailand_const_2007.pdf.

Kingdom of Thailand (1999), "Organic Act on Counter Corruption, B.E. 2542", www.oecd.org/site/adboecdanti-corruptioninitiative/46817329.pdf.

Kindgom of Thailand (1956), "Criminal Code, B.E. 2499", www.ilo.org/dyn/natlex/docs/ELECTRONIC/82844/120561/F-530967875/THA82844%20Tha.pdf.

Los Angeles Times (2015), "Thai trafficking crackdown targets corrupt police, officials", 8 May, www.latimes.com/world/asia/la-fg-thai-trafficking-20150508-story.html.

Marshall, A. (2014), "Thai police target human traffickers but rescued Rohingya may face more abuse", *Reuters*, 13 February, www.reuters.com/article/2014/02/13/us-thailand-rohingya-idUSBREA1C0FB20140213?feedType=RSS&feedName=everything&virtualBrandChannel=11563.

Marshall, A. and A. Sawitta Lefevre (2014), "Special Report: Flaws found in Thailand's human trafficking crackdown", *Reuters*, 10 April, www.reuters.com/article/2014/04/10/usthailand rohingya special report idUSBREA 3922P20140410?feedType=RSS&feedName=everything&virtualBrandChannel=11563.

Ministry of Foreign Affairs of the Kingdom of Thailand (2015), "PM declares 'anti-human trafficking' as national agenda", press release, www.mfa.go.th/main/en/media-center/14/55435-PM-declares-"anti-human-trafficking"-as-national-a.html.

Ministry of Foreign Affairs of the Kingdom of Thailand (2014), "Urgent Interim Measures to Prevent and Suppress Human Trafficking and Solve Problems pertaining to Migrant Workers, Phase One", Announcement of the National Council for Peace and Order No. 68/2557, 17 June, http://mfa.go.th/main/en/media-center/3756/46798-Announcement-of-the-National-Council-for-Peace-and.html.

MSDHS (Ministry of Social Development and Human Security) (2015), *Thailand's Trafficking in Persons 2014 Country Report*, Ministry of Social Development and Human Security, Bangkok, www.mfa.go.th/main/contents/files/media-center-20150311-164953-538433.pdf.

Office of The National Anti-Corruption Commission of Thailand (2015), "IOM Thailand and ONACC Entered into Cooperation Agreement", press release, www.nacc.go.th/download/article/article_20150721162548.pdf.

Prayut, O. (2015), "Speech by General Prayut Chan-ocha, Prime Minister of Thailand in the 3rd Conference on Evidence-Based Anti-Corruption Policy (CEBAP 3)", Bangkok, 17 June, www.thaigov.go.th/index.php?option=com_k2&view=item&id=92786:id92786&Itemid=398&lang=en.

Prompoj, W. (2015), "Combating IUU Fishing and Addressing Labour Issues in Thai Fisheries Sector", presentation, www2.thaiembassy.be/wp-content/uploads/2015/05/DOF-Presentation-Brussels-21-April-2015-final.pdf.

Sakdiyakorn, M and S. Vichitrananda (2010), "Corruption, human trafficking and human rights: The case of forced labor and sexual exploitation in Thailand", *NACC Journal*, www.nacc.go.th/images/journal/malinvisa.pdf.

Seafish (2015), "Focus on Ethical Issues in Seafood: Thailand Profile", Seafish Industry Authority, Grimsby, www.seafish.org/media/Publications/ThailandEthicsProfile_201509.pdf.

Szep, J. and A. Marshall (2013), "Special Report – Thailand secretly dumps Myanmar refugees into trafficking rings", *Reuters*, 5 December, http://uk.reuters.com/article/2013/12/05/uk-thailand-rohingya-special-report-idUKBRE9B400920131205.

The Guardian (2015), "Thai officials among more than 100 charged with human trafficking", 24 July, www.theguardian.com/world/2015/jul/24/thai-officials-among-more-than-100-charged-with-human-trafficking.

Transparency International (2011), "Corruption and human trafficking", *Working Paper* 03/11, Transparency International, Berlin.

UNIAP (United Nations Inter-Agency Project on Human Trafficking) (2009), *Exploitation of Cambodian Men at Sea: Facts about the Trafficking of Cambodian Men onto Thai Fishing Boats*, UNIAP, Phnom Penh, www.no-trafficking.org/reports_docs/siren/siren_cb3.pdf.

United Nations (2003), "United Nations Convention against Corruption", *United Nations Treaty Series*, Vol. 2349, No.42146, New York, 31 October, p. 41, https://treaties.un.org/doc/Publication/UNTS/Volume%202349/v2349.pdf.

United Nations (2000), "Protocol to Prevent, Suppress and Punish Trafficking in Persons, Especially Women and Children, supplementing the United Nations Convention against Transnational Organized Crime", Treaty Collection, database, https://treaties.un.org/Pages/ViewDetails.aspx?src=IND&mtdsg_no=XVIII-12-a&chapter=18&lang=en.

US Department of State (2015), *Trafficking in Persons Report July 2015*, US Department of State, Washington, DC.

ORGANISATION FOR ECONOMIC CO-OPERATION AND DEVELOPMENT

The OECD is a unique forum where governments work together to address the economic, social and environmental challenges of globalisation. The OECD is also at the forefront of efforts to understand and to help governments respond to new developments and concerns, such as corporate governance, the information economy and the challenges of an ageing population. The Organisation provides a setting where governments can compare policy experiences, seek answers to common problems, identify good practice and work to co-ordinate domestic and international policies.

The OECD member countries are: Australia, Austria, Belgium, Canada, Chile, the Czech Republic, Denmark, Estonia, Finland, France, Germany, Greece, Hungary, Iceland, Ireland, Israel, Italy, Japan, Korea, Latvia, Luxembourg, Mexico, the Netherlands, New Zealand, Norway, Poland, Portugal, the Slovak Republic, Slovenia, Spain, Sweden, Switzerland, Turkey, the United Kingdom and the United States. The European Union takes part in the work of the OECD.

OECD Publishing disseminates widely the results of the Organisation's statistics gathering and research on economic, social and environmental issues, as well as the conventions, guidelines and standards agreed by its members.

OECD PUBLISHING, 2, rue André-Pascal, 75775 PARIS CEDEX 16
(42 2016 09 1 P) ISBN 978-92-64-25371-1 – 2016

www.ingramcontent.com/pod-product-compliance
Lightning Source LLC
LaVergne TN
LVHW081417110826
845149LV00010B/1769
9789264253711